YOU ARE MORE THAN ENOUGH

Discover the light within you

Compiled By
Anita DuckWorth-Bradshaw

authorHOUSE®

AuthorHouse™
1663 Liberty Drive
Bloomington, IN 47403
www.authorhouse.com
Phone: 1 (800) 839-8640

Published by AuthorHouse 01/22/2019

ISBN: 978-1-5462-7618-0 (sc)
ISBN: 978-1-5462-7616-6 (hc)
ISBN: 978-1-5462-7617-3 (e)

Library of Congress Control Number: 2019900519

Print information available on the last page.

This book is printed on acid-free paper.

DEDICATION

To the men and women of the Powerhouse Global community, this book is for you. Thank you for your continual support of the Powerhouse Global Vision and Mission. Lady Anita salutes you. To my co-authors (Ross Swan, Victoria Andrew, Sarah Post, Adaobi Cornelia Oyekwelie, Antonia McClammy, Mina Kakaiya, Emma Di Gallo and Rossana Snee; you are highly appreciated for travelling with me, and supporting this project. Your contributions are the reason for the success of this project. I thank you.

*** **This book contains both British and American English. This is to keep the original writing of each contributor.** ***

Contents

INTRODUCTION

You are more than enough……..

I have met so many obstacles on my journey, and some who questioned my ambition to make real tough decisions in raising the bar for the next generation.

Well, it all starts with a journey of self-discovery and openness to embrace the endless possibilities life presents to me.

"Life is a journey and each one of us must start from somewhere, because where we are today, is a result of the journey we have made and the path we chose." – Anita Duckworth-Bradshaw

You are more than enough is a collective effort of high profile professionals who besides all their successful achievements, decided to share their story and insights in various topics with the world through this book. They have gone the extra mile to offer some powerful practical tips on several different topics, which will eliminate the thought of 'self-doubt' and promote positive attitude towards greatness.

These professionals are located in different continents of the world, and each of their chapter is loaded with information that would transform your life.

CHAPTER ONE:

Completeness by: Anita Duckworth-Bradshaw

In recent times there has been various news about people (celebrities included) taking their own lives due to not being able to cope with their challenges. Most of these individuals have everything money can buy. Some of them are at the top of their successes. We cannot say what actually got them to pull the trigger, or what their last struggles were before they took their own lives. Well, we can only speculate or make our conclusions based on their previous or much recent behaviours before they departed this world.

Some might call it depression, while professionals who are experts in dealing with such areas of human behaviour could call it something else. The news of 'suicides' cuts across the continents of the world (Africa, Australia, Europe, Asia, Middle East and America), they each have similar ending. They might differ in the way the acts were carried out, but they achieve the same result – taking their lives. This mental illness cuts across all spheres of life and influences. It brings me to ask the question; what is the solution to this epidemic?

I have come to the conclusion, that there is no solution outside of the person who is directly affected by the 'illness.' There could be a platform for 'managing the 'illness', but there are no lasting solutions outside the sufferer. Why did I say this?

Case study:

during my mental challenge, because at that period of my life nothing made sense to me. I was in so much emotional pain even though I was still serving the needs of others. Although, I never thought of taking my own life, but my mind became completely blank. I was unable to create at my best because my mind was blinded by my pain. I had to be strong for my son and those who looked up to me. In all of this, it took two people to call me to order. They reminded me of my brilliance and all the amazing things I had achieved in life so far. They even reminded me of how I supported them to do, have and become more than they were before meeting me. One question that woke me up from my depression was DO YOU KNOW YOU KNOW THAT YOU ARE A POWERHOUSE WOMAN? This was my wakeup call to my completeness.

"Our decisions of what to do are powerfully shaped by the emotions that we feel." Anthony Robbins

My decision to stop feeling sorry for myself was the beginning of my recovery. Fear and unworthy feelings prevented me from making decisions to be great again whilst I was in that state of mind. I instantly changed my limiting belief after the shake up by my very dear friend (AF). Nothing physically was given to me to help change my state of depression. All the solution to feel better was already deposited inside of my being. It only took a reminder from true believers of my greatness to awaken the sleeping brilliance in me. This confirms that 'you are more than enough' and much more. We all can heal again if we are ready and willing to shift our mind-set and dare to dream again even after a fall.

Our total completeness is within ourselves and no one can make us complete outside of ourselves. Everything we have and we would ever have (spouse, children, business, houses, cars, big fat bank account, rich influences, education, luxuries and all sort) are but 'COMPLIMENTS' to our 'COMPLETENESS'. By studying the pattern of the causes of 'depression', one discovers that the attachments to the above mentioned COMPLIMENTS are usually the reasons for mental and emotional breakdowns in our society. Perhaps we lost a relationship, we went into debt, lost a loved one to death, became homeless, lost a business deal or even laughed at by others - these are usually the triggers of the feel of failure, fear and inadequacy. It creeps in slowly as we focus on what we are going through, or what we may have lost in that season or period of time. Without noticing the changes in our daily behaviours towards our family, friends and work, we slip into that dark place of not wanting to carry on any more.

During my challenged period, I stopped worrying about my daily work output. I couldn't be bordered by anything. All I saw was tears and the situation that I was surrounded with. I felt physical pains around my chest area. It was like hot air in my chest – the tears were unending. Sometimes I would find a small corner on the street just to cry. No phone call would end without a cry at the other end.. No conversation was without tears as I try to explain my feelings to whomever was interested to listen. Nothing made sense to me and I just didn't care. All I wanted then was to make my pain to go away. All I wanted was to see an end to my challenge. Some of the people around me could not understand why my tears could not stop. They did their best to comfort me, but it didn't matter nor made sense. My best comfort was to cry. During that period whenever I cry; the hot air in my chest eases off a little bit. But still my challenge did not go away.

Depression is something that kills silently. People who are not trained to deal with this health challenge often think that the sufferers are only being difficult. But the only people who would understand the pain that such an individual is passing through, is someone who had been on that same or similar road. Some of these individuals come out fighting back, whilst others are not so lucky - they end their lives. Until I passed through the road of depression, I did not fully understand the reason behind the behaviour of those who suffer from such an illness. I was lucky to overcome my challenge due to my decision to keep living and making differences in my world. The will-power to change the direction to my destination was the beginning of my recovery. I have never written nor spoken about this until now.

"Every obstacle is an opportunity to create miracles." – Dr Wayne Dyer

It was due to my personal experience with depression that I created 'HEALING FROM WITHIN'. This is a programme designed to support the internal healing process of people who desire to better their lives irrespective of the storm that has hit their ship. In this programme I share key strategies on how to let go of things and people that no longer serve our purpose.

During my journey I discovered that we are already 'COMPLETE' and I recognised that every outside element is all 'COMPLIMENTS' to our brilliance. In most situations people who couldn't get over the loss of 'COMPLIMENTS', tends to forget their powerful nature (THE COMPLETE BEING). The complete being does not need outside compliments to function to full capacity. The complete being is already complete. It takes a deeper underastanding to know and believe this truth. Whether it's the loss of a loved one or other earthly possessions, the complete being does not change form due to the wind that blows. Rather the complete being becomes more (added experiences) as a result to the event that took place. Although, it takes a 'MINDFUL' person to embrace their completeness and walk in the actualization of their brilliant life – everyone can if they believe.

"You will never find the secret of prosperity outside yourself." – Dr Wayne Dyer

Like Dr Wayne Dyer explained in one of his teachings; he emphasised on the importance for us humans to understand our Spiritual nature. He also stated that we are more that the physical eyes can see. Humans are only sharpened by the happenings in the 'inside' of our being and not 'outside' of us. Because I was focussing on what was missing in my life and what I had wanted to 'be' during the time of my illness, I was unable to see the beautiful bold, intelligent, world changer and powerful Lady Anita. My inner eyes were only on my then challenging situation. Due to the mental blockage, I robbed myself the opportunity to see the personal growth which was taking place in my life during the process, until that moment when the wakeup question from my dear friend came heavily on me... It was as if my internal creative process was re-started just by that one act of bold question.

"You are already complete in all and nothing in the physical would make you more complete." – Dr Wayne Dyer

I was fortunate to have quality individuals in my circle of purpose who were able to support me during my challenge. So, that leaves us with the question; what happens to those without adequate support? What happens to those who are going through the motions of life storms? What happens to those who are too afraid to share their feelings without being judged or ridiculed? What happens to those who have forgotten how brilliant they were before hitting 'rock bottom."? My suggestions would be to constantly check on those whom you care about. Notice their behavioural patterns and call for help if you sense that they are in danger of harming themselves and others. You never know; you may be saving a destiny from going down the black hole.

As a leader and a certified life coach, I have conditioned myself to continual learning on how to do, have and become more on a daily basis. During my recovery process, personal and professional books and audio channels were my keys to taking bold steps towards a better me. Looking back now, I am grateful for the experience my challenge has given me. I know in most cases some people never recover from such challenges. However, there are possibilities for more people to get better if they have the right support. The very first step to living a fulfilled life is accepting who you are. Knowing that everything you would ever need to become the champion you were born to be is already inside of you. Until one decides to understand the uniqueness of one's being, the outside forces (things and other people) will continue to be in charge of one's thoughts and will influence one's decisions.

About the author:

Anita Duckworth-Bradshaw (Lady Anita Bradshaw) is the Powerhouse Global propagator. She is a certified life coach, author of 5 personal development books, a multi award-winning global impact leader, global speaker and trainer. Lady Anita is the President/Founder of Powerhouse Global Awards, Powerhouse Global Magazine, and the President/founder of Powerful Women Global Foundation Africa. In 2016, she fed over 400 children in Africa, and she has continued to carry out various charity projects on a yearly basis. Her passion to serve the need of others stem from her own personal journey, as one who struggled through childhood to becoming a voice in the global market. She is a great voice for women across the globe (those hurting and those living in fulfilment).

CHAPTER TWO

A Star Was Born

By Rossana Snee, MFT

A long, long time ago in a hospital far far away, a star was born. No, I am not talking about the 1976 film starting Barbra Streisand and Kris Kristofferson. Or the 1937 version, or the 1954 version. Or the 2018 version with Bradley Cooper and Lady Gaga. For some reason, this movie invites remakes. Perhaps it is because everyone loves a rising Star. Well, for the purpose of this chapter, that star was, is, and always will be you, not Lady Gaga or any of the actors who've risen to stardom singing their hearts out.

So, back to *a long, long time ago*...now that you know that I am referring to you, let's really get into it. I have a hunch that right about now you might be thinking, *Me, a star? Yeah, right! I'm no star. Everyone I know says so.*

I beg to differ.

On the day you were born, it was like another little star lit up the sky. It was beautiful, bright, and ready to shine in life. It didn't know anything other than to do its thing, and that thing was to light up the world with its presence.

Now, if you were taken home by caretakers whose light still shone brightly, then you were quite fortunate. Your parents, or whomever carried you home on that day, gave you more of their light and showed you how to continue to express yourself in unimaginable ways. You grew up knowing your place; knowing your capabilities. The world was your oyster!

But if you, the little star, was taken to a home—a home with limitations, hatred, prejudices, and ignorance—a home shrouded in darkness—run by caretakers whose light had dimmed way before you came into being, then your own personal light may have started to dim almost as soon as it arrived at its new destination; before it really had its chance at creating magic.

Keeping that brilliance is hard work. There is almost always something external, whether it's another person, or a hellacious situation, that challenges the vitality of that inner flame to keep it from shining outward.

Let's suppose that you come into this world full of hope, wonder, love, and ready to thrive. Just imagine that. Your caretakers, however, don't know how to feed that amazingness. Like an old light bulb, perhaps their light burnt out years ago and was never replaced. But here you are, ready to be You, to do what You do, to say what You say, and to express yourself the way you were meant to. Instead of a guiding light to lead you and make you shine brighter, you are met with hostility, anger, abuse, neglect, etc. What do you think would happen in such a situation? How would you be able to prosper in an environment like that? It would be quite hard, wouldn't it?

Here's what I want you to understand. If in fact, you were born to people who view the world in a very limited fashion, through cloudy eyes, and ideological misconceptions, then what you need to know is that it's not you who are the problem, it is them.

As a Licensed Marriage & Family Therapist, I've worked with many clients who were fed unbelievable lies by people who didn't know any better. They were abused, told they weren't any good, tormented, and kept from evolving into their best Selves. They came home full of life and enthusiasm, but the lies that had taken root in their minds started to eat them up, until little by little their shining spirit began to fade away, until one day, all they had was a head full of crazy stories, lies, and addictions to help them cope.

Here are some of the lies you may have heard:

NOTE: I'm not talking about lies that include, "*Yes, Virginia, there is a Santa Claus.*" "*The Tooth Fairy left you the money under your pillow.*" "*If you swallow gum, it will sit in your stomach for seven years.*" And so on. No, I'm talking about the lies that shape a person's psyche; lies that affect behavior and self-confidence. For instance:

- "You should never have been born!"
- "You'll never amount to anything."
- "You're responsible for everything that is wrong with our family."
- "You're meant to be seen, not heard."
- "Don't say anything to anyone. It's our family secret." (This could be referring to keeping a parental addiction a secret, or a worst-case scenario, physical and/or sexual abuse.)
- It's your fault!

These are just some of the lies that may have been programmed into you. Your mission, if you choose to accept it, is to re-program yourself so that the light that is hidden within you, can begin to glimmer, just like it was meant to.

In order to do that, you have to recognize that you were given misleading information growing up. Remember, you were brought home from the hospital full of hope, life, and ready to love and shine. You did not choose your parents, the country in which you were born, the city in which you grew up, or the religion that was fed to you until you believed that that was the Only Truth. Everyone else is wrong, of course.

All of these things were out of your control.

But you're an adult now and fully in control of your life. You can cease to let the past define you. It is only part of your history. It is not You! This re-programming may be challenging. After all, if you've grown up believing one thing and have acted accordingly, now at 33, 56 or 62, it may be difficult to delete all that garbage and start anew.

You can because You have the power to do so. First things first; know that you may have been fed a lot of rubbish. It may be stuck inside of you, so old and toxic, that eliminating it may seem next to impossible. But it's not. I have a garbage disposal at home. When I need to discard any expired or leftover food, I stick it in the disposal. I don't do it all at once, however. I put it in a little at a time, until it's all gone. That's what you need to do. Get rid of your junk, a little at a time.

Start small. Name one thing that you were told growing up that has never felt good; something that has caused you to doubt yourself; that has made you want to stay hidden. Once you have identified what that is, ask yourself, is it really true? Try to be unbiased here. If you don't think you can be able to overcome your challenge, ask someone you can trust, or a professional who is completely unbiased. Just because someone says something about you, doesn't make it true. It is just their opinion. And who are they, after all? Why does their opinion matter so much? Are they an enlightened human being? I personally don't think so; there aren't too many of those around. Mostly, there are people driven by greed, ignorance, and the need to control others. An enlightened human being would never have put you down in the first place. They would want you to evolve, develop yourself into your highest potential—physically, psychologically, and spiritually. Anyone who hasn't wanted that for you is not anyone from whom you would gain confidence, self-esteem, and self-worth. Instead, you would probably feel the opposite—insecure, self-doubting, and unworthy.

Okay, so now that you've made some assessments and have identified the one or several things that don't ring true with you, now what?

If the person who didn't allow you to shine is still in your life, if they're toxic, and see you as a failure, then you need to take some action; step away from them, for instance. **Words, spoken often and with conviction, can seem true even if they're not**. The mind is a pretty amazing thing. It is basically at your command. Whatever you or anyone else tells it on a regular basis, will be taken in, believed to be true, and acted out in accordance with that "truth." Especially in the early years, when more than 1 million new neural connections are created in the brain, every second that ticks by counts to aiding the functioning of a person. The years between 0 and 3 are quite critical. All the interactions that transpire during those formative years shape and have a long-lasting impact on the person. If those early experiences are traumatic, the more threatening the effects are to the emotional well-being long term.

Fortunately for you, there is hope. If you've been despairing up to this point, know that things can change. Here is some good news about your brain: It is plastic. It is at your disposal. You can make it change. Because of the brain's plasticity, it is quite moldable. Its neural synapses and pathways *can* be repaved, if you will. Yes, you read that correctly. Your behavior, your environment, the words you say to yourself, can create new pathways in your brain - New and improved. Isn't that great news?

Imagine a freeway. There are four lanes, but a new one is needed to allow ease of flow. With some work, a whole new lane can be built. This can open things up quite a bit, make things a lot better for that darn traffic congestion. So, by creating new pathways things can change for you as well. You will be creating an opening for goodness, for positivity, for open mindedness. It is then you'll have a chance to evolve into the person you were meant to.

If you want to create a brain that believes in itself, that feels confident in what its power is, then whatever you feed it has to be geared toward that. If you are continuously thinking negative thoughts, regurgitating lies that were fed to you; if you walk around angry and anxious, then that's all your brain knows. It can't do anything else, behave in any other way than what it knows and believes. Hence, why it's important to re-program it? If you start by saying, "I am good enough," "I deserve love," "I am worthy," then your brain will start creating those new neural synapses. It finally has something good to work with.

Because the brain has been fed lies for so long, it will take a couple of weeks to start believing the new information. That's OK. Be patient. Be consistent. There will be some naysayers who won't like the new you. After all, that may mean you're no longer at their beck and call. That's fine. You weren't born to be someone's slave. You were born to radiate out, not in, remember?

You may be wondering, *Well, how do I know who the real me is*? That's a legitimate question. If you were raised in a toxic environment and continuously fed untruths, then, yes, it would be hard to discern who the real you is. Here's a hint: the real you is that person hiding in the shadows; the one who wants to do something, say something, but doesn't because it is afraid.

Name a fear that you may have. For example, it could be: *I am afraid or I'm not smart enough to go to school.* In a case like this, you would ask yourself, "What/who made me think I wasn't smart enough? **NOTE**: **You weren't born believing this**. Ask yourself, "Was I ever told I was too stupid to attend school and get a degree?" If you were, make up a list called, **Lies I Was Fed,** and put it on the list. Or, maybe you are in a relationship with an abuser. Perhaps growing up you witnessed abuse in your family and thought that abuse was "normal." It is not! It never is. If you find yourself in a relationship with an abuser, do you believe that he's the best you'll ever get in life? If so, also put that in the **Lies I Was Fed** list.

Before we go on, I'd like to insert here some truths for you to ponder while reading this chapter. I want you to read them aloud. Once you've read the list over several times, memorize its content. Put little Post-it notes throughout your home and say them every time you spot one. Make sure you stick plenty of them around. Don't be stingy. This is your light we're trying make shine here, okay? Here we go. This is your starter list. Once you start to feel more confident, you may come up with your own.

- **I am perfect the way I am.**

  Here, I am talking about your essence. That part of you that never changes. That's the real you. Your exterior is constantly on the move. If you don't believe me, look back at your baby pictures. Now look at yourself in the mirror

- **I am more than enough.**

  And you are. If you want to add to what you already have, that's perfectly fine. Just saying, you don't have to, but you're welcome to go for more. I like your spirit.

- **I don't need to hide who I am.**

  You don't, unless you're a serial killer. In that case, you definitely don't want people to know where you hid your last body. If you're around people that make you want to hide, reconsider being in their presence.

- **I can do anything I set my mind to.**

  This is within reason, of course. If you're 40, you're probably too old to start training for the Olympics. What I'm talking about here is that anything, upon which you focus mind, expands. You set it in motion by your newly-programmed brain. So, choose what you want to set in motion, and then focus all of your energy on it. You will reap the rewards, guaranteed – unless you give up. So, don't!

- **I believe in myself.**

  This will probably be quite difficult. If you've been brainwashed into believing that you're not good enough, and that you're expendable, then believing in yourself won't resonate well. Believe that you are meant to be here. Because you are! There's absolutely

> no one out there that can take your place. Not a one. Not even your twin, if you have one.

Some of the above statements may seem like falsehoods. That's understandable. In fact, it's normal, especially if you've been raised to believe otherwise. Remember what I said earlier, "Words, spoken often and with conviction, can seem true even if they're not." The point here is to make a shift in your brain so that it no longer believes the urban myths that keep you stuck. The goal is to get your brain to see the truth so that you can start living the amazing life you were supposed to. This doesn't mean you're not going to have problems. You are. We all are; that's part of life. But with a strong belief in yourself, you will be better able to weather the storms.

WARNING: You may encounter quite a bit of resistance. And not just from an external source. The biggest resistance may come from you. You've been living with your brain and everything in it for a long, long time. There's a lot of stuff in there. Imagine having an email account. Let's say this account – ibelieveeverything@gmail.com – was created for you when you were one. You started receiving messages almost as soon as it was started. You scanned them daily, not comprehending everything, but taking in as much as you could, even the SPAM. Your little brain wasn't able to decipher the truth from the lies. So, you never bothered to delete any of the messages; never thought you had to. You just assumed that all the mail was valid and important. When you became older and finally decided to re-check your mail, you discovered that you had thousands of messages, and most of them *were* SPAM. But interspersed with the SPAM, there were some really good things in there. Unfortunately, those good ones in the mist of the SPAM were too hidden to be recognized.

In order to extract the meaningful and significant stuff from the junk, you'd have to go through all of those messages. Imagine how much time it would take to determine what's worth keeping, and what is needed to be deleted forever?

It is the same with the messages in your brain. There's a lot of junk in there and it will take some time to decipher what's valuable and what's not.

In the movie *The Help*, Aibileen Clark—a black maid in 1962, in Jackson, Mississippi, played by Viola Davis—lived in a world where orders were taken quietly. Where racism was prevalent, and blacks were considered less than others, Aibileen Clark was in charge of a little white girl, played by Mae Mobley, who was being raised by racist and bigoted parents. When the little girl was four, Aibileen Clark sat her down, and in an effort to teach her how wonderful she was, she said, "*You is kind. You is smart. You is important.*" Those were good words. If that little girl was able to retain those true and amazing words, there's a chance that she might believe that about herself, despite what else she may have heard to the contrary. Sometimes all you need is one good person; one person that can speak genuinely to you, and who loves and accepts you for who you are - one who wants to watch you grow into a beautiful human being. Start looking for that person today. There are good people out there that will recognize your uniqueness. Until you find that person, if you haven't already, what are some of the things you can do?

1) **Embrace and accept your uniqueness**. Don't compare your life or yourself to that of anyone else's. It's a waste of time. Just focus on yourself. No two people have had the same experience. And even if they have, their perspectives of the experience can be totally different. When I was in graduate school, one of my assignments was to interview our siblings and find out how they saw our lives as we were growing up. I have three brothers. Not surprisingly, each of them and I, had a very different take on our growing up, even though we were raised together and by the same parents. It's really like having

four different witnesses to the same accident. You're going to get four different versions. So, don't compare yourself to anyone. It's not fair to you.

2) **Be compassionate to you**. It's amazing how nice we can be with people out in the world, with virtual strangers, and yet be so cruel to ourselves. If you want to re-program your brain, you're going to have to work on this one. You have to start being nice to yourself, saying kind and positive things. Start becoming aware of the thoughts you have about yourself. If a negative one sneaks in, stop it from taking its next breath. Replace it with a nice one.
3) **List 3 great things about you**. When I was in high school, my psychology teacher had us go around the room, choose one person, and say something nice about that student. Whether it was that they had nice hair, a warm smile, or a winning personality. Everyone left that day feeling good about themselves. If you're thinking that you have nothing good to say about yourself, you're wrong. Dig deeper!
4) **Forgive yourself**. So, you've had a crappy life. And maybe your circumstances led you to do or say some things of which you're not proud. It's over now. Time to let it go. Forgive yourself. What is the point of holding on? If holding on makes you feel like a better person, you're fooling yourself. You can't be your completely great self unless you've let go of your guilt. Allow yourself a fresh start, free of your past, a past that no longer exists. I once spoke with a woman who, after 18 years, hadn't still forgiven herself for dropping out of school. To this day, she blames her current life situation, the present job she has (because she didn't pursue the other career), on the fact she dropped out. She keeps looking back, nearly two decades later and can't forgive herself for not having stuck it out. What good is this doing her now, 18 years later? I can tell you. It's doing her no good. Until she forgives

herself and accepts her situation now, she will not be free, or happy. She could make different choices now, if she chose to, but she's too busy looking back, blaming herself, and loathing the fact that she gave up. The first step is to forgive herself. Once she's free, she can start reviewing other options. Maybe going back to school is a possibility for her. She won't know until she allows her past to stay where it belongs.

5) **Speak up**. You aren't meant to live in the shadows. If you have something to say, say it. I'm not saying you can say whatever you want to, whenever you want to, especially if it will hurt others. Keep that to yourself. I'm talking about saying things that help you grow. Namely, talking about your desires, your dislikes; expressing yourself in your life without worry of criticism. Stop apologizing for your past. It's your past. You're in the Now. I was recently talking with a young man who told me he had very little confidence. When around people, he clams up; he's unable to say a word. He asked me for some advice. I asked him what it was that held him back from engaging others. He explained that he felt stupid, and that he was fearful he'd be judged and criticized. Like I said before, he wasn't born feeling that way. That feeling of self-doubt grew little by little because it was planted there by someone who didn't have his best interest at heart. Someone who wanted to silence him; someone who wanted him to be seen, not heard.

None of us gets to choose the moment of our birth, and all that comes afterward. All we can do is to live out our life situation to the best of our ability. Yes, sadly some situations are despicable. And until you can do something to get out of it, you have to bear it. For that I'm sorry. But once you become an adult and are free to walk out, drive away, and cut the toxic connections, you are able to change your life.

The most difficult part will be making a mental shift, creating those new neural pathways that will get you to where you need to be. You're going to have to work for this. But aren't you worth it? You may not think so now, but you most definitely are!

If you've had a pretty breezy life and haven't had to deal with horrible maltreatment, you're one of the lucky ones. If you had parents who cared and raised you to care for yourself and others, that's wonderful! Go out and help those who weren't as fortunate.

And if you are part of the group that got the short end of the stick, talk to your brain. Remember, you have to create a new belief system. You're going to have to convince your brain that you are worthy, lovable, and deserving of love.

I'll leave you now with my version of Aibileen Clark's (*The Help*) beautiful words:

You is Enough.
You is Worthy.
You is Lovable.

Now go out and prove it!

About the author:

Rossana Snee received her Master's Degree in Psychology from Antioch University in 1996. She is a Licensed Marriage and Family Therapist who has helped countless individuals re-direct their lives by providing them with healthier choices and coping skills.

Her goal: to empower as many people as she can. This is why she wrote: **The Healing Alphabet, 26 Empowering Ways to Enrich Your Life**—an easy-to-digest template for self-improvement.

In 1966, at the age of 8, Rossana Snee waved goodbye to her grandmother for the last time. In search of freedom, with only the clothes on their backs, her parents fled Cuba, flew to the United States, and made California their new home. There, Ms. Snee shares a home with her husband of 31 years, three dogs, and the parents responsible for her freedom.

Two amazing sons and four grandchildren keep her busy. But not so much so that it stops her from writing, painting, playing four different instruments, and teaching a fitness class at her local YMCA.

If you hear her talking to herself, don't assume she's crazy. She just might be practicing her French. Or Hindi!

Ms. Snee is currently working on **The Healing Alphabet 2, 26 Empowering Ways to Strengthen Your Relationship**—a couple's Bible for surviving the all-too-common relationship pitfalls.

Ms. Snee is live 3 days a week, (M, W, F), on Periscope (@ askjoshsmom), where she helps her followers with their relationship issues. She is also a monthly contributor to *The Lakewood Community News*.

www.rossanasnee.com

CHAPTER THREE

How to Boost Your Metabolism and Lose Weight

by: Adaobi Cornelia Oyekwelie (survivor of 5 cardiac arrest and Pulmonary Embolism)

There's a nasty rumour floating around out there that fat cells are permanent. And the nastiest thing about this rumour is that it's true. Yes, most experts conceded that fat cells once created are there for life. Yet this doesn't spell doom and gloom to those of us who could stand to drop a few pounds. Because even though experts believe that fat cells are permanent, they also agree that fat cells can be shrunk. So even if the absolute number of fat cells throughout your body remains the same, their size appearance and percentage of your overall weight can be reduced.

The bottom line is simply that metabolism represents a process of countless processes, in fact, that convert food into energy. When this process creates cells, it's called anabolism. When this process breaks cells down, it's called catabolism. For people trying to lose weight, it's important to experience catabolism. That is, it's important to convert food into energy that is used to break cells down.

Catabolism is also important because it prevents excess energy (calories) from being stored by the body. Remember when the body has too many calories regardless of what food source those calories came from it can only do two things. It can desperately try to see if you have any energy needs (like maybe you're running a marathon at the time). Alternatively, more often, it will have to store those calories. It has no choice. And unless you have lean muscle that is gobbling up those excess calories, you'll be adding fat.

The remainder of this book, however, is going to point you in the opposite direction. You'll learn various techniques, tips, and strategies to boost your metabolism and lose weight. And then, in the latter part of this book, you'll be introduced to some metabolism-boosting foods that you'll surely want to add to your regular eating regimen.

Tips, Techniques, and Strategies for Boosting Your Metabolism

If you're reading this book, chances are that you've tried at least once in your life to boost your metabolism. Perhaps (like me) you weren't quite certain what a metabolism was, and perhaps (again, like me) you probably didn't quite know all that you needed to know in order to accomplish your goals. Maybe you started a rigorous exercise program of jogging and muscle toning or maybe you started eating several small portions a day, rather than three large traditional meal sized portions or maybe you started taking all kinds of supplements that promised to boost your metabolism.

Really, exercise, eating strategically, and ensuring that your body has catabolism friendly supplements are but three of many generally good ideas.

So what's the problem?

The problem is that many of us have no real scientific understanding of what, how, or why these methods boost metabolism. Some of us, in fact, don't really even know if they work; we just think that they do. For example, a person may start a vigorous exercise program that includes significant aerobic cardiovascular movement, such as jogging or cycling. And indeed, after a week, that person may notice a drop in weight.

Yet is this due to a boosted metabolism?

Could it be due to water loss through perspiration that hasn't been adequately replenished? The point here is that many people are at risk to their health and wellness, and they don't quite understand the tips, strategies, and techniques of boosting their metabolism. And that's what we're going to rectify in this chapter.

In this book, you won't come across any casual information that a friend to a friend heard on TV. Nor will you be subjected to off the-cuff information of how to boost your metabolism. Rather, we're going to look at the popular, easy, fun (yes, believe it or not), and successful ways to boost your metabolism.

I've taken these 3 broad categories:

1. Exercise
2. Lifestyle
3. Diet

Exercise

It's going to be old news for you to be reminded that exercising is a bit part of boosting your metabolism and burning up calories. Unless you're born with one of those unusually active metabolisms which allows you to, almost freakishly, eat thousands of calories a day without weight-gain consequences, you're like the vast majority of us who need to give your metabolisms a bit of a kick through exercising.

Now, you might think that cardiovascular (aerobic) exercise is an important part of boosting your metabolism; and you'd be right. Provided that, of course, your qualified doctor confirms that you're able to start a program of cardiovascular exercise, this is indeed the place to start. Increasing heart rate, blood circulation, body temperature, and oxygen intake or carbon dioxide exchange all send messages to the system to initiative catabolism.

Build Muscle-Many people particularly some women are very wary about undertaking any exercise regimen that can lead to muscle building. The old perception was that muscle building leads to muscle bulking, and before long, gorging forearm veins and other unwanted results. This is, frankly, not the case. Provided that women aren't supporting their workouts with specific muscle-building supplements, there is no need to be concerned; because building lean muscle won't make them bulk up. Of course, as you can infer, if you build muscle and then leave it alone, over time, the muscle fibres will weaken, and you'll lose that wonderful calorie-burning factory. However, that's no problem because all you need to do is build and maintain healthy muscle. It may sound daunting; especially if at the moment you perceive yourself to have much more fat than muscle.

Yet the important thing for you to remember is that once you start building muscle through any kind of strength training your body will itself start burning more calories. It has to; even while you sleep, or go to a movie, or read a book. It's like putting your calorie-burning program on an auto-pilot.

Interval Training-The basic weight loss nuts and bolts behind cardiovascular exercise is, as you know, a matter of catabolism. Essentially, if you can engineer your body to require more energy, your body will comply by breaking cells down to deliver it; and that process burns calories. Simple, right? So based on that logic, something called interval training neatly fits in with the plan. Interval training is simply an adding high- energy burning component to your exercise plan on an infrequent, or interval, basis. For example, you may be at a stage where you can jog for 20 minutes every other day, and thus put your heart into a cardiovascular zone during this time.

This, obviously, is going to help you boost your metabolism and thus burn calories/energy disproportionately more calories if, during that 20-minute jog, you add a 3K0 second or 1-minute sprint. Why? Because during this 30 seconds or 1 minute, you give your body a bit of a jolt. Not an unhealthy jolt; remember, we're talking about quick bursts here, not suddenly racing around the track or through the park! By giving your body an interval jolt, it automatically and somewhat unexpectedly has to turn things up a notch. And to compensate for your extra energy requirements, the body will burn more calories. It's essential for you to always keep in mind that interval training only works when it's at intervals. This may seem like a strange thing to say (and even difficult to understand), but it's actually very straightforward.

The metabolism boosting benefits that you enjoy as a result of interval training is primarily due to the fact that your body, suddenly, needs to find more energy. While it was chugging along and supplying your energy needs during your cardiovascular exercising, it all of a sudden needs to go grab some more for 30 seconds or a minute; and in that period, it will boost your metabolism as if it were given a nice, healthy jolt. As you can see, if you suddenly decided to extend your 30 second or 1-minute sprint into a 20-minute sprint, you simply wouldn't experience all the benefits.

Yes, your body would use more energy if you extend yourself to the higher range of your aerobic training zone. But your body won't necessarily get that jolt that only comes from interval training.

Lifestyle

When we come across the term lifestyle, we tend to think of the basic day-to-day habits that we rely on; sometimes without giving them much of a second thought. And this is indeed the case when we talk about how lifestyle influences the speed of your metabolism.

Now, quite honestly, most of us live busy lives in one form or another, and therefore it's challenging to really keep an eye on all of our habits. Balancing work, family, hobbies, and other commitments means that our lifestyle isn't so much of a choice, as it is a necessity.

Yet with respect to the fact that many of us face sincere limitations in our lifestyle choices, there are many things that we can do little things, but important things that can help speed up our metabolism. So if you're a bit put-off by the term lifestyle, please don't skim over this section. The little things that you change in your regular, day-to-day lifestyle can indeed have the most profound. How to boost your Metabolism influence on the speed of your metabolism, and the achievement of your short and long-term weight loss goals:

Relax

We briefly noted yoga in the list of Things to do above, and that brings us to another key influence of your metabolism: stress. Believe it or not, but experts are now telling us that stress can send unwanted signals to our body; signals that lead to slower metabolism.

Essentially, what happens is that when the body is under constant stress, it releases stress hormones that flood the system. These stress-related hormones actually tell the body to create larger fat cells in the abdomen. The result can be both increased weight (through increased fat cells), and a slower metabolism.

Obviously, these are two very negative factors in the quest to boost metabolism and lose weight. The last thing that we want is more and bigger fat cells in our abdomen, coupled with a diminished metabolism.

Yet this is, tragically, what happens to many people who experience constant, continuous stress. And, alas, this is many people; especially those of us who have to balance so many competing objectives, such as work, family, and other vital tasks. So the advice here is indeed to "relax and chill out", and there are some simple techniques that can, and should, be added to your life.

These include walking more, listening to relaxing music, meditation, yoga, eating non-stimulating foods, and building a daily regimen that includes periodic time outs where you can re-centre yourself and de-stress. So if you don't want to relax because you don't have the time, then you should realize that your stressed-out life is probably playing a role in your weight gain/your inability to lose weight.

Some non-medical tips to help you fall asleep include:

- Don't eat late at night
- Try drinking warm milk before bedtime
- Don't turn on the TV at night
- Try yoga or other stress-relieving practices
- Try having a warm bath before bedtime
- Don't exercise close to bedtime; your body can become so energized that it doesn't want to sleep.

There's Something Good about This Time of The Month

Now here's a strange one that is for the ladies, only. Studies have demonstrated that the 2-week period prior to the onset of PMS is one in which fat burning capacity is at a premium. This is ironic indeed; because that's usually the period in which women don't want to work out; because their body and its emotional computer are preparing for PMS. However, studies in Australia have shown that women were able to burn off as much as 30% more fat in the 2 weeks preceding PMS. The reason for this, researchers argue, is because this is when the female body's production of estrogen and progesterone are at their highest. Since these hormones tell the body to use fat as a source of energy, exercising during this time can really pay off. The body will be inclined to target fat cells for catabolism.

Diet

For most of us, our information concerning metabolism has related in one way or another to eating. Most of us have been told of metabolism-friendly foods, or metabolism unfriendly foods. But really, while we may be basically aware that, all else being equal, a stalk of celery is better for your metabolism than fries with gravy, our understanding of diet and metabolism is pretty low.

About Adaobi Cornelia Onyekweli:

Adaobi is currently most known for her extraordinary near-death survival. Her story is well known by top cardiologist surgeons and medical doctors around the world as she shattered several medical records to still be alive here today.

Has been featured in or interviewed by several media outlets such as Powerhouse Global Magazine, and several social media influencer, all within the past few months of being discharged from hospital.

During her serious health crisis, she was put in an induced Coma (24th December 2017 – 30th January 2018, she also suffered the following:

- 5 cycles of Cardiac Arrest, in 5 days
- 2-Month Coma/Life Support
- No brain activity for 1 month whilst in coma
- 01% Chance of Survival
- Multiple Pulmonary Embolism
- Multiple Organ Failure
- Liver Haematoma
- Blood Clots
- Sepsis
- Full Body Rehabilitation

And she is now learning to walk with 2 Crutches! Her Doctor's call her a Miracle.

Her Story

On the morning of December 24th 2017, I woke up about 7a.m, got up to brush my teeth on a very normal day and within minutes ended up in a coma for the next 2 months.

During that time, I experienced what I call "crossing over into another realm". In this realm, I had an incredible peace and happiness and did not know or remember life about being on earth, I had no separation all. I saw my siblings' faces those people who I have had some issues with and the funeral ceremony.

In this spiritual consciousness and I found myself in a classroom where I experienced lifetime reviews and my life and was being flashed to me on a screen. They were very displeased with me and refused me entry as I had been wasting the opportunity to make a change on earth. I made a deal and practically begged to be given a chance to come back and make this change.

My story is already changing lives as I have used my acquired knowledge, tools to support those with various life challenges. I am able to turn family, individuals, troubled teenagers, feuding neighbours, burn out executives with what God told me was important in this existence.

CHAPTER FOUR

Don't Steal Your Own Authenticity By: Ross Swan

Good leadership starts and ends with self-leadership. That is; you cannot lead people or influence people if you can't lead yourself. You need to be very visionary to lead people, you need to take them along on a journey, but you need inner vision to lead yourself and take yourself on a journey, which is where it all starts. What is your purpose? What do you want to stand for? What is personal brand? These are the questions you need to ask yourself to lead yourself and others.

This is not a simple process, as children growing into adulthood, deciding on the purpose can be more about what other people think, not what you know in your heart. Mainly this is because you are not fully aware of what life is all about, and therefore the big picture for you hasn't quite jelled yet. I have seen young adults with a burning passion to follow a particular path from a young age gone on to become high achievers in their chosen field. They achieve because they have a clear purpose.

For far too many people a clear purpose in life doesn't come easily. Not determining your own life's purpose means you are influenced by outside sources to help fill the void, such as parents, teachers and friends, cultural environment around you and the list goes on.

It is a known fact that some people are so called 'lucky' enough to fall into positions that they enjoy, whilst others are not. In all of this, I believe it's not just luck, but it's most likely to be their sub conscious attracting what is right for them. I believe everyone has a chosen path to lead but sadly many people never discover it and it's their self-talk that buries it.

You need to tune in and listen to yourself and not be influenced by outside chatter. You should be asking yourself what is important to you. This starts by being truthful to yourself. Not what's important to you based on outside influences, but what is your own personal burning desire that's just your own thoughts. This is where your self-talk is so critical. You have to be really honest in what you tell yourself.

A good friend told me this story that shows what I mean.

She told me that every morning she caught the bus with her partner; the bus driver greeted her partner but not herself. Initially she was thinking that doesn't matter. That moment the mind created a reaction of "oh it doesn't matter", "he doesn't greet me that am great, that way I don't have to greet him back" that's easy for me. She was trying to put a positive slant on what was happening.

Over time she realised that she is lying to herself. On a permanent reflection, the fact that she never was greeted by the bus driver really did bother her. Why does my partner get the greetings and I don't?

She was lying to herself, telling a lie to yourself for something as simple as that can prevent personal growth. How many lies do we tell ourselves daily? If the situation isn't important you may let it go and that's fine. But be clear in whether it's important to you or not. I am sure we have all experienced situations like this. An accumulation of 'not important' can lead to problems in the future. Yes! Do I let it go or is this really important to me? Be truthful with yourself

In not being truthful with yourself, what you are doing is stealing your own authenticity.

In the midst of an uncomfortable situation, where a part of us is afraid to face the truth, our mind quickly tries to stir us into a space of safety through self-deception or blaming others.

With self-awareness, it is possible to detect what is going on – either by being mindful of one's thoughts or by engaging the body's wisdom through self-talks as a gauging tool.

Have you ever noticed how your body reacts when meeting someone whom you feel uncomfortable with? Compare that with the physical response when bumping into your best friend. There is always a physical reaction to thoughts and emotions. Our body doesn't lie and can be of great help if we take the time to become attuned to it and care to listen to what it has to say. It can be a great ally to question whether what the mind wants us to believe is right for us at that moment.

In the business world, often leaders are taking action based on from too much outside influence rather than what their inner self calls them to do. Sure, we need to take counsel and be flexible, but do so when you feel its right to do so. Playing the political game, fulfilling other people's expectations, competition, or achieving a particular social status is often more important than what rings true deep within themselves.

Being honest with oneself keeps one out of that loop. Being aligned physically, mentally and spiritually one brings forth integrity and authenticity into leadership for both yourself and for others you influence.

Find Your Bravery

Beyond our body we are wrapped in an energetic field, others often pick up quickly when we are not in alignment with our thoughts, emotions, and body. They may not be able to put a finger on what they sense, but their body picks up on the incongruence in that field, making the person feel uneasy and at worst not trusting. Often our body language gives us away too.

To be able to do so genuinely, courage is needed for us to establish our most crucial primary relationship, a relationship with ourselves. That is connecting with your inner self, your soul.

Being at peace with one's various aspects, even the ones we would judge as undesirable will provide consistency and balance in our messages. Accepting the expression of all aspects in a balanced way makes each unique in personality, characteristics, and vibration. It makes it easier to trust ourselves, knowing that we are more than OK.

Having a robust and stable connection with ourselves, our Inner Self, creates the foundation to connect with others on a much more meaningful level.

The eyes as a window to the soul offer a beautiful way to be with each other, soul to soul. To connect through the eyes to the heart, to be seen and heard acknowledges the other person as a human being with their journey, their narratives, facets, and qualities.

To quote my good friend Kimberly Davis; most times it takes bravery to do this. It allows you to be vulnerable because you are dropping your guard which not only allows you to see who you are, but it allows others to see who you really are as well. **That's the Brave Leadership** which we have discussed with her on one of Soul-Inspire-Leadership podcasts.

When one feels, sees and hears, it acts as an invitation to follow from the heart, and most likely we choose to do that because we want to, not because we have to.

This is crucial in the workplace. Employees who know they are seen as significant contributors, with valued ideas and perspectives, who can co-create and live their purpose, want to come to work and their discretionary performance is harnessed. When leaders are connected to their mission, their legacy and can communicate that positivity to their teams, these also enable them to work towards that purpose.

"This feeling within yourself, that recognition of your own truth, and finally saying it and expressing it, is such a great feeling! It helps you to have the courage to be true to yourself."

The same goes for how you look at others. It's recognising other people's own truths and not making snap judgments with all the biases and outside influences around you.

Bias is everywhere in daily life, especially in the workplace.

Instead of judging people, from a preconceived set of ideas or *perception*, you should assess people with the view of learning something that you are not aware of.

Leaders assess their employees. Such assessment can have filters of being biased which are as a result of your own perceptions. This then could culminate in a judgment.

Perceptions are built very much based upon the experiences we have had in life. Our upbringing, our programming, our culture in which we have been brought up or we live in and our values all feed into how we see ourselves, how we see others and how we see the world.

So, the question is how do I prevent myself from judging or seeing the world through my filters?

It has to do with awareness. The idea would be to question oneself. Is what I am seeing or what I am perceiving really the truth?

The first thing in finding the truth is to accept that we all have our own perceptions. Therefore, our perception of a situation or someone's achievements or their skills may be completely different from that of another person.

How does one bridge this and work through it?

Perceptions form with a lot of activity and input which then gets narrowed down as you make assumptions and experiences add on different things over the years. It forms the bias we carry. We are biased in the areas of hearsay, people saying something about someone else and you take on board this opinion and you haven't even met the person yet. Yes, you can listen to what you are hearing and use it as background knowledge but don't allow it to formalise you own opinion. This is bias because it's someone else's perspective; that you are displaying by judging and putting them into a specific frame where they don't necessarily belong.'

It's a challenge, as a simple bias can cause all sorts of problems as you go through life, particularly affecting leadership in the workplace. It creates all sorts of negative energies and which then affects performance.

People put facades up as a protective mechanism for insecurities for all sorts of things.

The key is to get under that guard and talk to the real person and good leaders can do that because they are trying to extract the real value out and grow their people. It's connecting with people's inner self and this happens when you can connect with yours.

In working through bias, one needs to take a step back and try to look at the bigger picture.

It's trying to see people for who they really are in a broader way, rather than the most obvious way. It is also important to broaden our view and see the world or a certain situation for more than it is rather than just through our own little lens.

Whilst it's easier said than done, good leaders ask good questions because questions are the sign of an enquiring mind. It communicates that they value a person's opinion which also helps with their connection.

Always look for value in people, a sign of good leadership. Firstly though, you should be looking for the value in yourself. Appreciate what you have, no matter how small you perceive that to be, and build on it. As mentioned before, your self-talk is the most powerful tool you have for succeeding in your purpose.

Everyone has value. Good leaders bring out the best in people. They are always looking for how they can grow people and how they can bring that person out to be the best person they can be.

Self-leadership is doing the same thing by working on being the best person you can be.

The key is awareness and being open to self-reflection and asking yourself so what else can I learn from wherever I am because everything in our lives is really an invitation to learn more about ourselves.

It's a matter of having the patience and being brave to go against other people's perceptions and discover your own perception. Discover yourself from your own assessment and self-evaluation.

As mentioned don't give up in looking for what is positive and then build on it.

Serve Others To Serve Yourself

In leadership circles, there is a lot of talk about servant leadership. Servant leadership is a leadership approach where a leader has a facilitating and serving people mind-set. It's an approach where the leader sees his or her role as serving the team and not the position. That also rings true in your own life. Of course, you cannot do that at your own expense totally. It's about creating a balance.

Such a mind-set creates high energy levels within a team who, usually, have a collaborative vision or bigger picture and move towards achieving that. This enables a more effective performance. Likewise, on a personal level people will respond to you in a much more positive way.

Some of the things that help you become more of a servant leader personally, is seeing how other people live and becoming more appreciative of who you are and where you find yourself... A way to do this is through voluntary work.

The moment you step into voluntary work you start realising that there are many people who are far worse off than you. At the same time, the activities help us get in touch with parts of ourselves that we may not have yet faced and tend to humble us and put us in a mind-set of serving. As we learn more about the information we were not aware of, we tend to get a better understanding of ourselves. This awareness impacts our perspective and changes our perception. It helps a lot to see how you see your own life and the lives of others.

Serving the community creates a mind-set of helping people and you will see the rewards and value of doing so.

In the workplace, there's no difference when you're leading a team. You get rewards and value by serving them as the team will respond because they are being recognised and appreciated for who they are and for their struggles, not just merely as an employee.

As in doing voluntary service, the servant leadership behaviour at work is the same because you are looking from the perspective of I'm here to serve people and learn from them even if their circumstances are challenging, I'm still learning from them and it's adding to my self-development.

The designated leader provides the vision and goes ahead in clearing the way and then moves aside. Collaborating and supporting them in the daily functions but stepping back allows team members the space to perform and be recognised. That is the servant leader mind-set, which is based on the function of being a leader and not on the function of being a positional leader. Behaving in the same way on a personal level has the same effect with people growing and achieving around you.

Mindfulness… good for the soul

In today's life, we are continuously bombarded with information. Our brain not only has to take in the data but also sort it so that it makes sense to us. Add to this the monkey mind, and we are heading towards stress, brain fog, indecision, and energy depletion.

Therefore, it is crucial to develop the capacity to allow the brain to relax, not to scramble so that we can be 'here and present'.

Mindfulness is being present in the moment making it easier to discern which information is relevant to us. This discernment isn't possible being 'in the mind', but definitively more natural to achieve by being 'aware of the mind'.

"Wisdom and purity (of the mind) are accessible if we can get out of our own way."

A couple of minutes of reflection a few times a day for leaders are the go-to solution to find those needed answers – putting all the clutter aside, being open and receptive to insights and information from the subconscious.

Albert Einstein once said, "We cannot solve our problems with the same thinking we used when we created them."

Challenges in life can be an essential step for transformation and growth if we can resist rehashing the incident in the same old loops of our mind. Taking a step aside to assess quietly, with neutrality, will help gain different perspectives and new insights. We can then incorporate old learning with new ideas to climb up life's ladder.

When things aren't going so well we default to the mind to solve them. When things go wrong, a solution needs to be found to prevent the same mistake from happening again. Ideally, these rules and regulations are then combined with awareness in the present moment in case a similar error occurs to be able to react out of the box.

Rather than following the rules blindly, presence in crisis enables one to access a different stream of consciousness and therefore offer creative solutions for the better.

While the conscious mind can process 7 bits of information consciously, the subconscious mind has access to 7 million bits of information. Being able to still your mind, achieving clarity, is a skill to have to access the subconscious mind and those 7 million bits of information. Being mindful and conscious of what is happening within you is the key to stop your energy leaking to the wrong areas.

One "easy" way of getting into this state of a clear mind is regularly taking the time to sit still and observe one's breath. You need to breathe anyway – you may as well do that mindfully.

Stopping our energy leaks

Everything we do each day takes energy. Effective leaders know how to focus their energy so as not to drain themselves. When we focus on what we want from within it gives us strength. When we focus on everything around us that spreads our energies too thin and often drains us and our energies go.

"It is your choice how you react to things." Apart from reacting wisely the idea here is to become increasingly aware how people, situations or thoughts, drain our life energy on a continuous basis without us even realising.

As I mentioned before it is essential to allow yourself time during the day to "reflect on how you are going today? What are your challenges? How do I feel at this moment?" This helps you to control what happens during the flow of the day, so you can be proactive, rather than constantly reactive to the stimuli around you.

This daily check-in balances, and saves, a good percentage of your internal energy. The things you do either give you energy or drain you. Choose wisely.

The more you engage in things that you are good at, and like, the better you become, the more your energy will increase and vice versa.

A good leader can identify the uniqueness in themselves and within individual employees. They are able to do the needful to help turn any downward spiralling energy around. Once the employee recognizes their energy drains and can "plug" them, their energy and motivation will increase. This change will be systemic, in that, the whole team becomes so much stronger as well.

How do we identify these energy leaks? Being mindful and conscious of what is happening within you is the key.

It is your choice how you react to things." Apart from reacting wisely, the idea here is to become increasingly aware how people, situations or thoughts drain our life energy on a continuous basis without us even realising.

Your self-talk

As mentioned before it is essential to allow time during the day to "reflect on how you are going today? What are your challenges? How do I feel at this moment?" This helps to control what happens during the cause of the day, so you can be proactive, rather than constantly reactive to the stimuli around you.

This is your self-talk, always be conscious of what you are telling yourself. Being aware of the destructive power of your negative thinking and balancing it with more positive perspectives is essential to our overall wellbeing. You do need however to critique yourself but be constructive not destructive. It's our choice to feed our mind, choose wisely. Inner truth as the foundation of one's decisions is a cornerstone of great leadership. I am not saying that you need to be selfish by only thinking about yourself, if you truly are seeking inner truth your thoughts will take in all perspectives.

This daily check-in balances and saves a good percentage of your internal energy.

The more you engage in things that you are good at, and like, the better you become, the more your energy will increase, and vice versa. Have it radiated out to power your day.

We all have an energy field around us which stores a vast amount of information, dating way back into childhood and even into our ancestry. In Energy Medicine, the necessary work to balance volatility or other issues happens mainly in that field. Scientists also call it the information field. Energy Medicine People tune into this field intuitively, fine-tuning their skills through meditation and inner work.

The more we understand ourselves, the more we steer towards inner and outer balance. Being in touch with oneself, acting from that intimate place of balance and serenity, fosters the authenticity previously mentioned.

When we develop this balance, volatility starts to reduce, intuition increases, and we observe and act from a higher level of awareness, which is inclusive.

For my clients, who embark on the journey of self-discovery, it is important to note that these changes in patterns and responses often happen over a period of time, are subtle and won't come with a bang most of the time. Some clients don't even notice the change unless they are prompted to reflect on their old behaviours.

Knowing your inner and outer ego

When we talk about connecting with your inner self and having a positive belief in yourself, you could ask these questions: Am I being egotistical? Ego is a positive thing for people and yet can be negative as well. Too much ego can lead to arrogance and not enough ego leads to insecurities. We do all have it.

Inner ego is the inner belief or inner strength that a person has. It is purpose based and it's connecting with your inner self. Outer ego is when you are driving yourself to be better than others.

Let's look at the outer ego first, it is in this space that people compare themselves to others around them and feel good about themselves by feeling superior or winning.

Alternatively, when your self-talk becomes negative, you don't see yourself as superior but inferior as problems arise. The inferior belief it still outer ego because you are comparing yourself with others, their expectations etc.

In a workplace, it creates challenges because people compete. Competition is healthy but quite often people compete with each other creating stressful scenarios and tension. Each one often times is trying to get the upper hand for a personal gain, and not necessarily what's best for the team. This can be classified as bad leadership and lack of team Spirit.

For instance, you have people who don't collaborate because they want to be winning and in control and will only collaborate when the purpose suits them and not the business.

Apart from collaboration, a siege mentality can sometimes surface. This is where leader controls a team and sets them apart and above everyone else. The culture is one of usually arrogance and leads to misalignment with other teams. Everyone has their own take on things and relate it back to themselves. How they see success, or how they want to be a success, it's usually at the expense of others.

Then there is the situation when you have an undeveloped ego, which is, feeling insecure about yourself compared to others. As a protection, you then may over compensate by appearing to be confident and strong without a balanced view of things and when pushed, act defensively to protect the insecurity.

From a coach's perspective, people who are unaware of the impact their ego has on others are usually easier to coach because once they are made aware of their behaviour it's a revelation to them and they work on modifying their behaviour. Unfortunately, there are people who are clearly aware of their behaviour and see it as a power game.

The challenge here is not just getting them to realise the stress and problems they create, but to have a desire to tackle the problem.

Success comes here when I manage to have them truly connect with their inner being, their soul. That's when they can clearly see their vulnerabilities and true desires. Once this happens, then they can start to build something more meaningful.

Having little outer ego doesn't mean to say you don't want to win, it just means you don't have to compete with others for gratification. You want to be in your race, to set your own standard, and your own desire on what you want to achieve, and you concentrate on beating that, not beating other people. If you ask yourself whether you are jealous of someone else's success? That is a good sign that your ego is not truly healthy because your emotions are triggering an inferiority feeling.

I have spoken about ego here with only a few examples because there are literally thousands of situations where it's the driver.

What you need to do is ask yourself where your ego is situated. Mainly coming from your inner self or is it always out there competing with others.

It's your inner ego that gives you the best view of the world. A healthy inner ego gives you that inner strength to be able to handle life's challenges. Develop it and you develop yourself. If your self-talk is undermining you keep looking for strength, no matter how small you may feel they are, and use them to be your foundation. Remember if you think they are small strengths that's only because you are comparing them in your outer ego space. It is important to keep to your inner thoughts in order to grow yourself from there.

The problems of this world manifest from people battling with other outer egos. Connecting with your inner self is a positive experience, and staying true to it, radiates out positive vibrations. Ask yourself, what do I want to be known for, my positive vibrations or for my negativism? It's your choice. It's your soul, no one else's.

So, in summing up I am ending with where I began, it all comes back with managing yourself, believing in yourself and your own self-leadership, remember that you need to lead yourself before you can lead others. You need to be in touch with yourself before you can connect with others; you need to understand yourself before you understand others.

And when it is all said, you need to believe in yourself and what you want to do in life, what you want to achieve, what is your purpose and stay true to that.

When others look at you and say, "don't do that, that's a bit risky" or "I don't agree with that" don't be influenced, if you believed in it then you decide. Only you control your destiny and only you know what's best for you.

About Ross Swan:

Ross is a perceptive and responsive leadership consultant, coach and trainer, with broad experience in varied industries worldwide, including financial services, construction, energy, beauty products, logistics, distribution, retail, engineering, hospitality, airlines, and manufacturing. He focuses on helping Leaders reduce their stress in managing people

Ross is also a dynamic speaker and podcaster with outstanding skills in communication, presentation, training, team-building, and interpersonal relations.

He works internationally with his projects encompassing many diverse cultural backgrounds.

Throughout the years, Ross has developed a growing desire to put an ongoing emphasis in bringing more soul into business and he believes that the most effective leaders stay true to their authenticity by being soul inspired.

You can catch Ross at www.soul-inspired-leadership.com

CHAPTER FIVE

In Praise of the Small Businesswoman

By: Victoria Andrews

During my time as a practising chartered accountant, and over the last two years as a small business adviser, I have travelled the same road as my clients. I have sat with some of them and supported them when they were reduced to tears by problems they were facing in their businesses, and I have worked with them to turn their businesses around. I have also rejoiced to see my clients glowing with satisfaction when their businesses became successful. A chartered accountancy practice can also be a small business, so I have experienced the same challenges and rewards as my clients. Over the years, several common themes and issues keep coming up, and I would like to share some of these with you later in this chapter.

Female business owners often have an additional set of challenges which I too have faced: these challenges may include how to balance childcare, care of elderly relatives, and other domestic responsibilities with the demands of the business. That is not to say that our brothers never take on these challenges, but statistically, it is still more often than not the woman's lot. The strength of women and the amount they manage to fit into their lives never ceases to amaze me, and being one of you, I guess I amaze myself!

How I started

Although I did my training with a big city firm of chartered accountants, with big city clients, it was always my intention to work with smaller businesses. Therefore, after I gained my qualification, I worked for a number of smaller practices to accumulate the necessary experience. Although starting my own practice was always part of the plan, it gained momentum when I returned to work after the birth of my son and discovered that my employers were not sympathetic to any form of flexible working. When my son was admitted to hospital aged nine months with a chest infection, there was no question in my mind that my place was by his side. I was prepared to make up the hours of work at a later date, or take the days missed out of my annual leave entitlement, but it was abundantly clear that the that only way that combining work and motherhood was going to work for us as a family, was to work for myself. There have been plenty of ups and downs over the years, but it has been a decision I have never regretted. I attended most of my son's school concerts, plays and sports days, and no-one can take that away from us. Yes, it sometimes meant working until 2am to meet deadlines, but it was really worth it.

What I can share with you about running a small business

Many small businesses cease trading in their early years. One set of statistics put this at one in three within the first three years of their life. How can you reduce the likelihood of failure?

Have a plan: every business should have goals, and that means you as the business owner need goals. If you are a one-woman band, you and the business are one and the same. Do you know where you are going? Do you know why you are doing it? Your goals need numbers: how much? When? For example, you might want to aim for a certain level of sales or net profit for each of the next five years. Many business owners do a business plan when they are first starting out, or when they need to borrow money from the bank. The business plan is then filed away and never looked at again. Having set your goals, you then need to continually review them against your business's performance. Always bear in mind that making a plan is a fruitless exercise if the plan is not implemented. It is well known amongst business advisers that one of the biggest causes of business failure is having a strategy but not implementing it.

Know your target customers: It is easier to work out future outgoings than it is to calculate projected sales. Market research is important, as is keeping an eye on the profiles of existing customers and noting any changes. You should also monitor what your competitors are doing. You can learn from them – what to copy and what to avoid. Do you know if your market is growing, staying the same, or decreasing? Do you know why your clients buy from you? If a potential customer does not place an order, do you ask them why?

Look after your Existing Customers: A customer care policy is vital because, if a customer feels badly treated by you or your staff, they may take their custom elsewhere, and what is worse, they will tell other people. Apparently, unhappy customers tell more people than happy customers.

You can improve customer care by asking your customers for feedback and acting on anything negative. Every business receives complaints, no matter how much effort the proprietor and staff put in. You will never manage to satisfy all of the people all of the time. Therefore, the way you handle complaints is important, to ensure that complaining customers will continue to use your business and will give positive reports to their family, friends and associates. Hear the person out before you make any comment. It makes a difference to people if they believe they are being listened to. Express sympathy and ask questions. Suggest a solution and if this is acceptable to the customer, follow it through, then contact the customer to ensure they are satisfied.

As well as good customer care minimising negative publicity, there are three positive results of looking after your customers:

- Existing customers may want to buy more from you (if their first purchase wasn't a genuine one-off).
- You can receive testimonials from satisfied customers, which you can then use on your website or other publicity material.
- Customers can introduce new clients to you (referrals).

Sell more to existing customers

There may be untapped sales potential among your existing customer base. Make your customers feel valued and take the time to understand their needs. They may follow your recommendation to buy a more expensive product, than the one they were considering if that product better suits their needs. If it is appropriate for your business, think about offering existing customers a loyalty discount for buying more from you. This is where insurance companies fall down; new customers often get better quotes for the same risk than existing customers renewing.

Reputation/word of mouth is the most powerful of all sales tools. Take every opportunity to seek out testimonials from your satisfied customers. A testimonial is a written recommendation from a happy customer confirming the performance, quality or value of a product or service. All testimonials should fit on one side of A4, end with a thank you, sound genuine; be genuine, contain specific and enthusiastic praise, read as if unrequested be addressed to you as the business owner, (not "To Whom It May Concern").

Have a system for obtaining customer feedback; not only is this essential for customer service reasons, it will supply you with a stream of positive messages which will open up opportunities for collecting testimonials. When you've just made a client happy, you should have a process and a script for turning great feedback into a written testimonial. Your happy customer is not going to provide you with a testimonial without being prompted. You might get a good review on social media, or on your website (if you have a space for feedback), but it is a fairly random process and there are no guarantees. Having a system in place will also get around the problem of customers being busy, and writing your testimonial could be at the bottom of their to-do list. Part of your system can involve asking the customer if they would like you to draft the testimonial, for them to approve. You can then give their feedback the best possible angle, while still of course remaining true to what they said. Happy customers will very rarely say no to a verbal request for a testimonial, especially if they do not have to write it! In fact, I once had this happen with a client, before I knew about having a system; I asked him for a testimonial, and he said, “Sure, but can you write it for me?”

Generate Referrals from Existing Clients:

Building your business through personal recommendation is the most cost effective and reliable marketing method. In my experience, once my accountancy practice was established, up to 95% of new clients came via referrals from existing happy clients. Although many referrals are provided by enthusiastic customers doing so proactively, without being asked, many more referrals could be generated, if firms actually asked their customers to refer work to them. Most of your customers have their own concerns about running their businesses and personal lives, so they are not automatically thinking about helping you to grow your business and get more customers. They need prompting, which is why you have to ask. If you don’t ask you don’t get! Some business owners are reluctant to do this. Maybe they don’t want to appear desperate or pushy. However, the evidence from those firms who do ask their customers for referrals is that the customers recognise that referrals are important to any developing business. Most people like to help other people, so assuming you have helped them through your delivery of an excellent product or service, you will not come across as pushy. Another reason that business owners are reluctant to ask for referrals, is that they don't know when or how to ask. There are three good opportunities to ask for a referral: strike while the iron is hot:

- When a customer says "thank you"
- When a new customer signs up or places an order
- When a project has just been completed.

The best way to ask for a referral is to be polite, professional, sincere and direct. Giving your business cards to your customer makes it easier for them to pass on your contact details to others. Be specific by letting your customer know the type of new customer you are looking for (e.g. industry sector and size) and the type of goods or services you are looking to provide. Avoid a vague request, e.g. "If you hear of anyone who might need our services, I hope you will keep us in mind." Whilst this is better than not asking at all, it does not create the clear picture of the businesses you would like referred to you nor what you are asking your customer to do on your behalf. The worst that can happen if you ask for a referral is that the customer says 'no'. That's not the end of the world or your relationship with them.

Finally, think about referring business to your customers. A great way of encouraging your customers to refer business to you (especially if you have asked them to) is by referring business to them. If you are thinking of purchasing goods or services, think about whether one of your customers provides what you need. In addition, think about which of your customers may complement each other, then offer to introduce them.

<u>Networking: Referrals from people who are not your customers</u>: Small firms need to establish and nurture partnerships and networks. Collaborating with other small businesses can help win new customers for both parties. Business networking sometimes gets a

bad press. However, when approached with the right attitude and done properly, networking will help to grow your business and have a positive impact on your life. Once you get into it, the experience can be enjoyable and rewarding. Successful networking is not about attending receptions in the vain hope of meeting new clients, nor is it about pretending to be someone you are not. Networking is the process of building reciprocal business relationships with people you like, admire and trust. Nurturing your existing networks is a good place to start. Trying to meet new people from scratch is difficult, whereas asking people you know to introduce you to their contacts is relatively easy.

Connecting with people via social media is all very well, but nothing beats getting out there and meeting potential customers, and people who are in a position to make multiple referrals to you. For example, when I had my accountancy practice, I focussed on developing and nurturing relationships with independent financial advisers, letting agents and small business bank managers. Networking is a skill that needs to be learnt. Most good networkers don't start out enjoying it; their "spontaneous" one-liners are rehearsed.

There are two types of networking, formal and informal. Formal networking covers organised groups such as BNI, Ladies Who Latte etc., and networking meals arranged by local banks and chambers of commerce. These organised events can be very productive, but you have to put in at least as much as you get out. I have never regretted the eighteen months I spent as a member of a formal networking organisation. However, there was a considerable commitment in terms of time and money. The financial outlay paid for itself many times over in terms of new clients introduced to me by other members, but I found it difficult to balance the time I spent on the organisation's activities with the time I needed to do work for my clients! These days I practise what I call, "informal networking" whereby I use my networking skills without attending formal events.

If you are going to attend a networking meeting, it is important that you do some advance planning. Find out who will be there and format of meeting. Prepare a good, short pitch (sometimes called an elevator pitch). Bring business cards. Arrive early for the meeting. It will be calmer, quieter and easier to find other people who don't have conversation partners. Find someone to start a conversation with. Ask easy questions. Talk about the event, then ask people about themselves, then talk about their business - ask about issues they are facing. Listen more than talk. A networking meeting is not a place for you to do your sales pitch. Networking is all about relationship building. Become good at small talk. There is no need to do the hard sell within minutes of meeting. However, you can talk enthusiastically about your product or service. Ask your conversation partner the best way to stay in touch. After the meeting, follow them up, and then follow up again.

The backbone of informal, (as well as formal) networking is the one-to-one meeting. This can be with a potential customer, or someone in a complementary business to yours, who is in position to deliver multiple referrals to you. It needs a system to work properly. Here are some tips for a good one-to-one meeting:

- Set a time, date & venue: your premises or theirs.
- About a week before the meeting, e-mail one another an information document about your own business, containing a brief outline of yourself and the business, a description of your most recent few customers, the type of people you would like to meet, where to look for referrals, your core products/services, your USP.
- Bring the same document to the meeting that you e-mailed the week before. You can also bring other materials that will help you help each other (e.g. business cards, leaflets).
- Spend an agreed length of time to talk about your business: aim to learn as much as possible about how to find referrals

for the other party. Use the information documents as a way to get started.

- Outcome: both agree at least one referral that you will each find for the other.
- Schedule your next meeting (at the other person's premises).

The holy grail of networking is the referral. A referral is a personal recommendation. It is an opportunity for a network contact to present their business to someone who is in the market to buy their product or service, where that presentation will be looked forward to with anticipation. The potential buyer must be expecting you to call, so your network contact must have spoken to him/her first.

Other opportunities to get referrals might include: an attachment with your invoice, a request after your e-mail signature, and recommendations on social media, educating your friends and family so that they become part of your sales team.

People are more likely to look for referrals for you if you have given them a referral. Therefore, you need to find referrals for others. Listen out for a need from someone you've you met. Tell the individual that you know someone who can provide that product or service and the business card of the person you are referring and ask if it is ok for them to call.

<u>Controlling Costs:</u> Look at each category in your profit & loss and consider where savings can be made without adversely affecting your business. Doing even just one of the following will improve your bottom line:

- Do you need to rent business premises? If you do a lot online, working from home, or using a co-working space could prove more cost-effective than leasing an entire building. Meet your contacts at their premises or hire a meeting room only when you need one.

- Stock can be managed and distributed by Amazon, which may be cheaper than having your own warehouse and delivery service.
- Be more energy efficient; making a small saving today will reduce next month's utility bill, while a complete overhaul of your energy usage could really reduce long-term costs. Reducing the office temperature by as little as one degree could cut your heating bill by as much as 10 per cent. Review your energy supplier(s) each year to make sure you are getting the best deal.
- If you spend a lot on paper, stick to storing documents digitally (with a back-up of course) and stop printing e-mails (I am guiltier than most!). If you must print, do it double-sided. Such changes multiplied by the number of personnel in your firm could save a huge amount of paper each year.
- Talk to your accountant about ways to minimise your tax and national insurance bill. Do you have the most efficient business structure for your level of profit? Trading as a limited company can give rise to savings, but it won't work for everyone. Some business owners might be better off converting from a limited company to a sole trader or partnership.
- Do more online: this could be as simple as replacing mail outs with e-mail, or a more major change such as reducing retail space by selling online. Another change you could consider might be switching from landline telephones to a VoIP service.
- Consider your commercial waste charges: the mantra here is "reduce, re-use, and recycle."
- Avoid recruitment agency charges by getting existing employees to refer new people, for an incentive which can be

far cheaper than agency fees. (Apologies to those of you who run a recruitment business!)

- Find the right person for the job, even if it takes longer. The costs of hiring the wrong person can be damaging to your business's reputation and to the bottom line.
- What about outsourcing certain activities? Do you actually need a permanent employee, or can the work be done by temporary staff or independent contractors? This will probably work out more expensive on an hourly basis, but the total annual expense may be less, as you are only paying for manpower when you need it. Check HMRC's guidance before you do it; they really don't like "disguised employment," and penalties for getting it wrong will soon eat into your savings.
- Think about your business vehicle(s). It is not always true that buying a car through your company is the most cost-effective way to get a vehicle for business use. It is often more tax-efficient to purchase the vehicle personally and claim HMRC's approved mileage allowances rates when using it for business. You can also save on vehicle fuel by using a fuel card.

<u>Nurturing your relationship with your bank</u>: Many business bank managers have disappeared from high street branches (in fact may high street branches have themselves disappeared!) But you can still keep your bank informed. Send them your business plan, and its updates, and not just when you need to apply for funding. In addition, annual accounts and, if you have them, management accounts, will show the bank that you are serious about running a well-oiled machine, and give them confidence in you.

<u>Pricing, margins and discounts</u>: Pricing is a compromise between cost, quality, demand and competition. Set your prices to cover your fixed costs, plus the cost of making each sale, plus a profit element. I once had to explain to a client who had made a loss in her business. I

also explained to her that not only had she not earned anything that year, but she had actually paid for the privilege of working!

When setting your prices, you do not have to match your competitors. If you offer a better product or service, customers will pay a premium - provided they know that your offering is better.

Someone once suggested that I double my prices; I would lose half my clients but would do half the amount of work for the same turnover. It was tempting, but in the end, I couldn't bear to have so many disgruntled ex-clients!

Giving discounts is fine if you get something in return. Give customers a reason for the discount and be clear what you want to achieve. For example, I used to give clients a discount off their next fee if they introduced a new client. If you set a time-limit on discounts, you can then identify the financial effect. Repeat the discount if the effect was good (until it stops working). If the effect was bad, you have learnt a lesson and the discount have come to an end.

Managing cash flow and credit control: Profit is very important when running your business, but good cash flow is vital: you need more coming in than going out. You should always be able to identify at any time who owes you money and how old the debt is. Assess every new customer's financial standing before extending credit, have payment terms in place, and adhere to them strictly. Invoice promptly, clearly stating when payment is due. Unfortunately, it pays to be tough. Extending additional credit to a bad payer in the hope of retaining their custom is a slippery slope. Be strict about not taking new orders from them until they have settled their bills.

Your business plan should include a cash flow forecast; an up-to-date version will show your known and estimated future outgoings, and the amount of sales receipts (not invoices) you need each month to ensure a positive cash flow. Have a system in place to chase money owing from customers and consider factoring your invoices to generate extra working capital.

In Conclusion: I hope that you have found these tips useful and will be able to apply some of them in your own businesses. Please treat the ideas as a menu, not a comprehensive to-do list; otherwise you will have no time left in your day to sell your products or services! You need to find a balance between working **<u>in</u>** your business and working **<u>on</u>** your business.

To all small businesswomen reading this, I would like to say: we are all amazing. We juggle the different parts of our lives, not always with ease, and not always with complete success, but always with strength and determination. We have nothing to prove to anyone; we have already achieved greatness, and we are great role models to the women of the future.

About the author:

<u>Vicky Andrew Biography</u>

Vicky Andrew was born in 1960 and grew up in Carshalton, South London, and on the Fylde Coast in Lancashire. She gained her degree at Somerville College, Oxford, where she met her husband, Mark, whom she married in 1986. After a couple of changes of direction whilst studying, she qualified as a chartered accountant with Coopers & Lybrand (now PwC). The birth of her son Alex in 1993 and a desire to work with smaller businesses led to Vicky setting up her own accountancy practice in 1994, which she ran successfully for 22 years. She now works as a small business consultant.

Vicky is passionate about supporting small businesses and enabling small business owners to realise their true potential. As a small business owner herself, she has a real insight into the challenges faced by her clients, but also the rewards which can accrue to the owner of a well-run small business.

Website: <u>www.vickyandrew.com</u>,

CHAPTER SIX

Nothing Just Happens by: Antonia Michele McClammy

Trusting God's Plan and believing what he said in his word: "My thoughts are not your thoughts, nor are your ways my ways," says the Lord. "For as the heavens are higher than the earth, so are my ways higher than your ways and My Thoughts than your thoughts." Isaiah 55: 8-9 NKJV

When I think about my journey I praise God for showing me that NOTHING just happened in my life. I am an ordained child of God. When I was born on March 7, 1967, I was made perfectly as God saw fit for me to blossom into a beautiful woman. I didn't know I was going to be the skinny and long-armed young girl with long hair and dreams as wide as a football field. I dreamed countless thoughts as I looked out that small window in my room. My parents were too strict in our household. Although I do understand as young children we needed structure but sometimes an umbilical cord can cut your oxygen off if you know what I mean. I always found myself staring at the kids playing kickball or stickball in the street… We were would have been lucky to go play with our friends on a few occasions It really depended on my parent's mood if I could sit on the porch or maybe indulge in a game of hopscotch or jacks… There were many times in my life I felt very sad and lonely in a family of five. My parents drummed constantly in our heads about getting our education. I started reading at a young age and one of my favorite authors then were Judy Blume and Charles M. Schulz all the time. I found refuge in walking to the library. That was one place I could go to all the time.

I thought I had a great sense of humor, but I felt insecure because the kids at school teased me. They always told me that I was ugly. Can you imagine this stigma that was put on me as a young lady? It was challenging growing us, but I decided to be a better individual as I journey in life. I did not experience much love during my childhood, but God has and continued to be faithful to me.

It's something how you can identify at an early stage what love is supposed to be. I remembered listening to my 45's such as O Bryan by You and I, Endless love by Lionel Richie and Diana Ross and Close to You by Diana Ross.... I was certainly a hopeless romantic person... I listened to those records until I could listen to them no more, because they were all scratched up LOL... At that point, I dreamed about my future and love interest through music. Music was soothing for my soul. It was my spa and escape time from all the madness in my young life. It leads me to wonder why I was here on earth... I didn't know my voice or my purpose I always felt lost.

Let's speed up the story: I thank God for his love that was infused into my life. When I got pregnant at the age of 16, I was confused because I didn't know what to do. I remember asking myself; what am I'm going to do with a baby? I was already 3 to almost 4 months gone when I knew that I was pregnant. So it was too late for an abortion. My inner soul wanted to give my son away for adoption. I wrestled with these thoughts if my son tried to find me and say momma, why did you give me away? I looked up and lifted up my hands to God to ask for his help. Lajuane is now 34 years old and he has blessed me with 3 beautiful grandchildren D'Marcus, Daliyah, and Avyah.

When I turn 20 years old my mom was diagnosed with breast cancer… She had an operation to remove the cancer in her breasts. Unfortunately, the doctors were not successful in removing it all… Months later the cancer spread to her brain and she had spinal meningitis. This was the saddest time in my life because I was about to lose my 38-year-old mother… Her life was just beginning it was certainly too early to end. I remember when I visit momma at the hospital… I didn't know this was the last time I was going to see her in a healthy state. My mother told me she was sorry and she loved me very much. Those kind words are embedded in my heart...

I share my youth story because nothing just happens in our lives. Although I have experienced so much adversity in my life, but I knew that I was destined for greatness. Should we feel sorry for ourselves because of obstacles or do we just roll up our sleeves and say "I got this"? I knew that I will be a better woman, mother, grandmother, and businesswoman as I travel in life. So the irony of my story is to keep a great tribe of supporters in your circles. Stay positive no matter how dim your light is in your life. Remember your story is always going to have a happy ending.

I love these slogans Work Hard & Play Harder and Your Vibe attracts your Tribe. If you want to conquer fear, don't sit home and think about it - just grab success with both hands. Anything you infuse in your mind is going to be successful. Think about all the seeds that were planted by our mentors, parents, friends, loved ones and the list goes on… No matter the challenges you endure in your life you are not your past. We are not our parent's demons. So remember nothing just happen in our lives just because of anyone else. You are destined for greatness because you were told you are special, unique, and beautiful. It's time for you to respond to all the voices of positivity in your head, and know these are messages from your father above. If you will answer the knock and honor the chance with discipline, creativity, urgency you may find yourself and your time.

My life is a detriment that your past doesn't determine who you are going to become no matter what you go through…

Chant this message: Yes I am a transformer. Yes, I am free from anxiety and stress that I may find rest in your father loving arms. Stay Focus and Keep the faith!

Mark it down: things do not "just happen." There is a God-arranged plan for this world of ours, which includes a specific plan for you. By Charles Swindoll

About Antonia M. McClammy:

Antonia McClammy is a visionary marketing consultant and CEO for the business Inversion Social Marketing Management (ISMM). I have mastered many years of marketing and building strategic and creative goals for small businesses and entrepreneurs. Antonia has managed social media and curated content for marketing in several companies and non-profits such as: Momentum Jaguar, Nationwide Insurance, FEMWORKS Communications, Forward Ever Sustainable Business Alliance, Trauma to Triumph Non-profit, Urban Souls Dance Company, Meoka Pilates, Houston Institute for Culture, Newark Business Hub, The Ferrell Phelps Talk Show and her latest project Teacher Confidential. My accomplishments include publishing ISMM Social Media Magazine, an instructor teaching Social Media and Marketing Classes for Small Business Alliance and Rutgers Business School CUEED program with the Newark Business Hub. I continuously teach social media marketing to small businesses staff, entrepreneurs, and in the fall of 2018 she will be publishing a book called Social Media Blueprint to Success. Antonia has an entrepreneurial mind-set, and spirit. Her experience in growing small businesses and Non-profits branding presence in media and communications, designing websites, and understand precisely how important your brand presence is in the media world. She continues collaborating with FEMWORKS Communications Agency with major marketing projects such as: Newark Arts Council, TedxBroadStreet, Apollo Theater, Recognize Newark, Status is Everything, Newark Small Business Summit, Newark Global Shapers, Newark Business Hub, Forward Ever Sustainable Business Alliance, Rutgers University Newark and currently working with Corporate Sisterhood Empowerment Tour based out of Houston, TX. Antonia understands the mind-sets of marketing and social media for Media & Arts Professionals, Authors, Coaches, Talk Shows, Social Initiative, Ministries and Small Business Marketing needs. Antonia is a graduate of University of Phoenix majored in Small Business Development and Marketing. She's 20 year resident of Houston, Texas and proud mother of one son and 3 grandchildren.

CHAPTER SEVEN

Identify who I AM – Formation of Identity

By: Mina Kakaiya

Are we who we think we are?

We all enter into this earthly realm birthing into a world of great diversity, observed within humanity the natural world and the universe in which we are surrounded by. We are all born with our own unique set of predisposed identities and specific conditions linked to our physical being and mental qualities. As babies and toddlers, we have no real awareness of our identity or the origin of our existence. Our identities around gender, skin tone, intelligence, innate talents and abilities that we are all born with, are initially formed by the cultural and behavioural norms, values and beliefs of our families. Other outside factors of wider social and financial circumstances, culture, language, religion, educational opportunities, political persuasions and life experiences also critically contribute in moulding our identities.

The dictionary definition of identity states that '*it is who you are, the way you think about yourself, the way you are viewed by the world and the characters that define you*'.

As much of our initial identity is shaped and influenced by our family's cultural beliefs, values and traditions and by wider societal cultural norms and practices such as marriage and having children, or carrying on the family profession or trade. For some, identities are formed by the illness or disabilities that they are born with, or by ones they develop over time. For some of us, we are pressured to adopt identities that others may want us to have, or we are being encouraged to go into specific career pathways or roles. These are often carved out or influenced by parents, or by people or peers who we feel were important to us at the time. Examples of this are entering into gang culture, forced marriage or even being coached or mentored by patents to harness a particular talent. For instance, tennis champions, sisters Venus and Serena Williams were coached by their father from a young age!

Life shows us that we are all varied human beings that think, feel and behave from our own individual stand point. Each person will have their own unique way of identifying themselves as sisters, brothers, friends, colleagues, single or co-habiting, lovers or partners, divorcees or widowers.

Whether we are aware of it or not, in this world of variety we naturally make judgements on our fellow human beings on things such as the clothes they wear, the car they drive, wealth and status, race, religion, gender and age, shape, size, appearance and behaviour. Whilst these personal preferences help us to know what we want and do not want, it also helps us to create new desires and identities within us. It can also separate us from others knowingly or unknowingly. Often this can lead to divisions between certain individuals or groups of people that can potentially be harmful in the case of religious intolerance, stereotyping and labelling. For instance, the emergence of social media has become a platform from which we present our identities to the world, to which some aspire, envy or feel they are not good enough.

These disconnections can distract and confuse us on who we think we *should* be, rather than who we want to or *can* be! It can also prevent us from experiencing the varied perspectives from the billons of humans who share this planet with us. Our interactions with others enable us to make choices about those things which bring us sadness and pain or joy and happiness. Our identity becomes the shackles of conditional living.

Can you imagine if we all looked and thought the same and had the same experiences? The world would be a boring place without the opportunity to learn, expand from the variety each of us has to offer for a new growth of ideas, solutions and unlimited creativity.

For some people life experiences catapults their identities away from family or wider mainstream societal or cultural beliefs, norms and conditions. That being said, for *all of us* the journey of identity is very individual and personal – it's an exploration of how we view and fit into this world. It's a journey of self-discovery in finding new preferences, desires and needs which we either resonate with, or reject in order to create our very own unique identity which is unlike any other. We see the world from only our own perspective.

As we go through life, whether we are aware of it or not, our identity is constantly evolving and changing. We are forever becoming something new from the very life experiences that spearhead us to acquire identities over a lifetime. Some of these identities we are born with, and others we have a choice to shed, develop or adapt into. Our multiple identities are not just interdependent on the life experiences and the choices we make to create them, but can be moulded by individual and collective beliefs and values that we hold about ourselves and the world around us. This includes wider factors such as money, work, physical and mental health, cultural influences and physical environments that give us greater purpose and meaning to the world.

Sometimes, our identities are adapted or changed when we or people we know experience changes in their relationships, physical or mental health, bereavement, loss, or trauma. In some instances, it can fundamentally alter our core belief systems, values and attitudes that we have about ourselves and the world around us, into something greater or lesser then who we think we are.

When I was asked to write a chapter in this book, I had to alter my own predisposed belief systems in order to adopt a new identity of being a writer. A year ago, the idea of becoming a writer was something that was not a part of my identity. It helped me to shift my identity as a writer by altering my beliefs of being a writer. I drew on my past experiences of success in recently writing an article on the 3 waves of wellness in the Powerhouse global magazine as well as completing a Masters a few years ago. This gave me the confidence to believe in myself to be a co-author. In all honesty, when agreeing to write this chapter I had no idea on what I would be writing about! But with a bit of patience and faith, the ideas began to flow.

So as different experiences and opportunities are encountered on a daily basis, the question is *"how willing are we to shift our beliefs of who we think we are, to who we think we can be?"* If we can allow ourselves, then perhaps we are able. More often than not, we are all so wrapped up in our past or present conditions of life and beliefs, and due to this negligence we often fail to see the forever evolving beings that we are. If I had held negative beliefs of fear and doubt, and not believing in myself that I can write, I would have not discovered or unlocked the potential to express the words you are reading now.

I would now like to take you through a journey of self-discovery and to give yourself permission if you want, to briefly unlock the 'unconditional loving you' and the true essence of who you think you are by temporarily taking off the conditional, multi-faceted layers of identities which we have that define, serve or hinder us. We are going to imagine unpeeling these identities like layers of an onion. As you mentally read and go through the different layers of yourself, it is important to be non-judgemental, honest, kind and loving with yourself. Stop and take some deep breaths where you need to. Perhaps have a paper and pen at hand to note down what comes to you if you want.

Let's begin. Relax by taking a few big, deep breaths in and out.

The Body identity is the first identity given to us at birth, and we become more self-aware of our body by the age three. We are born into varied shape, size, height, skin, hair and level of physical and mental health abilities. Our body changes and carries us over a lifetime. The body identity is an awareness of being able to respect and honour it in the best way we can. What does your body mean to you? How do you look after your body? Are you able to accept it and love it as it is right now? Are you able to give thanks to it and its intelligence of keeping you alive? Breathe into this and notice what thoughts and feelings come to mind. Be kind, honest and loving with yourself.

The Gender identity is the second identity given to us followed by a gender specific name. In some faiths like Sikhism, gender neutral names are often given to both sexes. Genetically, we are both males and females as we all have both sets of chromosomes with slight genetic variations that differentiate the sexes. For women particularly, their gender identity is strongly reinforced biologically when they go through the menstrual cycle, pregnancy and menopause.

As humanity evolves so also does the definition of gender. I reference the term pangender, which refers to people who do not label or feel that they identified themselves to any specific gender. Now, become aware how you feel about your gender and as you peel off your gender identity temporarily, breathe into this and notice what thoughts and feelings come to mind. Be kind, honest and loving with yourself

The Age identity has differing cultural connotations across different communities around the world. For some, older age is associated with slowing down or becoming invisible in society. For others old age brings passing of wisdom and cultural traditions, whilst the younger age bringing forth new wisdoms and solutions.

For some, old age is about reinvigorating one's life and challenging the myths surrounding it. For example, individuals who are aged in their seventies and eighties are running marathons, or young geniuses exhibiting amazing mental abilities. Whatever age we are, be it 10 or 100, the beliefs we hold about our age determines how we behave and choose to live our lives. Are you willing to let go and become ageless? Is age linked to as old as you feel? Now become aware of how you feel about your age and as you peel off your identity of age temporarily, breathe into this and notice what thoughts and feelings come to mind. Be kind, honest and loving with yourself.

The Colour of your Skin identity - Initially we are all given labels to a particular group linked to the colour of our skin or race. Some of us tend to not integrate or relate to groups outside our race or ethnic groups due to cultural, religious or wider societal influences, and or even personal preferences. The question is how strongly do you identify with the colour of your skin right now? Does it challenge you or present you with any barriers? Do you like the colour of your skin? Does it bring feelings of pride, shame, indifference or non-relevance? The truth is that we exist within a multi-coloured world of people with many shades of skin colours. However, are we truly able to see our fellow human beings beyond their skin colour, racial differences and stereotypes? Are you able to see yourself beyond the identity of your skin colour? Whilst we are varied in skin colour and tone, something that we do share in common, is that we *all* belong to one race - The human race.

Again, become aware how feel about your skin colour. As you peel off your identity of skin colour temporarily, breathe into this and notice what thoughts and feelings come to mind. Be kind, honest and loving with yourself.

Sexual identity Regardless of your sexual orientation or preferences, human sexuality has been under significant cultural and religious persuasion and moral judgements, particularly where homosexuality has not been practiced as the norm. This has led to intolerance and hatred resulting in many individuals leading secret double lives. Some have been imprisoned, murdered, or have taken their own lives.

So, how do you feel about your sexual identity and expressing your sexuality? How has your sexuality defined you? What feelings of different sexual orientations evoke within you? Do they create unity or separation from yourselves and others? Are you able to see people beyond their sexual orientation and preferences?

So notice what thoughts comes to mind as you peel off your sexual identity temporarily, breathe into this. Be kind, honest and loving with yourself

Religion or Faith identity - Many of us are born into families who follow a particular religion, faith or belief system. For some of us, challenging or changing our birth faith or religion can be perceived as taboo and has led some to being ostracised from their wider family unit or wider communities. Whether you are a Muslim, Hindu, Sikh, Christian, Buddhist, agnostic, atheist or any of any other self-identifying faiths, think about how these labels and identities make you feel. How attached are you to them? What practices, objects, books or symbols link you to your particular faith, religion or belief (if any)? It may be the Cross, Om, Khanda or crystals. Or specific clothing or practices you observe such as dreadlocks, turban or hijab.

How close are you to this identity? Is there room to breathe? Is there non-judgement here right now? Be honest with yourself and ask yourself *"are you able to accept others' differing opinions? Are you open and tolerant towards others' beliefs and faiths?"* Maybe you no longer identify with the particular faith or identity you were born into. Or perhaps you connect more strongly with it now than ever before. Are you able to let go of this particular identity linked to religion faith or belief temporarily? Notice what this may feel like for you before you choose to put this layer back on. Breathe into this and notice what thoughts and feelings come to mind. Be kind, honest and loving with yourself.

Political Persuasions -We all hold at some particular political beliefs or persuasion on the way our communities, societies, countries and the world are governed at a micro and macro level. Some of us have freedom of speech to challenge and vote for the governance of our countries, but many do not. Whatever your political persuasion - whether you lean towards the left, right, centralist, liberalist, socialist, communist or apolitical - who are the figures you admire? What is the creed, qualities and belief systems behind the political cloak you wear? Historically and currently political and religious persuasion has caused some of the biggest geopolitical problems around the world, causing confusion, division and fear amongst societies. It has also inspired peaceful solutions, compassion and harmony amongst communities and nations around the world.

Feel into your political persuasion and know that it is just another layer of your identity that enables you to experience and view life in a particular way. If you have no political alliances how does it make you feel? It is only one aspect of who you are, not the whole. Like the seasons, politicians and public opinions come and go. Trends and beliefs come and go. They change over time as we all continue to evolve. Notice how your political beliefs are weighed down by judgement, division and misunderstanding. Do not judge it; just observe the feeling that comes with it. Is it weighing you down or giving you a sense of freedom? Breathe into your political persuasion and notice what thoughts and feelings come to mind. Be kind, honest and loving with yourself.

Culture, Race and National identity - We are all born into a specific country, race and culture. Whether we are French, Indian, British, Chinese, Mexican, Russian, Canadian or American, many have migrated from their country of origin to another. Some of us are now third and fourth generation descent and of multi- heritage, cultures and faiths. How do we resonate and feel about the country we belong to? Some may feel pride and love. Others may feel disappointment. Breathe and feel into detaching from your identities of culture race and national identity momentarily with balance and non-judgement. Notice how this feels before you put back or let go of some aspects of these identities. Be kind, honest and loving with yourself.

Name identity- Our name is a choice that was made for us. We are given a name at birth by which we are all known by, most of the time. Some of us have nick-names, middle-names or have performance/stage names. Some are referred to by many different names. I have a friend who is referred to by three different names by family, formally and through his performance/stage name. Your name has been called many times and you have answered to it many times. How do you feel about your name? Do you like it? Would you like to change it? Notice how you feel temporarily without your name. Would anybody still know who you are? Breathe and feel into detaching your name momentarily with compassion and non-judgement. Notice what thoughts and feelings come to mind. Be kind, honest and loving with yourself.

Relationship Status identity –This is formed and can change over a lifetime. As we live our life, our relationship status can either change or stay the same through choice, or if it is imposed upon us. Some of us are single, married, divorced, widowed or separated. How do you feel about your current relationship status? Is it one of lack, loss, duty or loneliness, or is it of happiness, contentment and appreciation? Notice what it says about you and how important is it to you? What do you feel about yourself and other people's perception of your relationship status? Now breathe and imagine having no relationship status. How does that make you feel? Be kind, honest and loving with yourself.

The Family identity- We are all born into a particular birth family. Some of us have struggled or thrived within our family identity. Some retain strong healthy life bonds, whilst others have been adopted or become distant and estranged from their families. How does it feel to let go of your family identity temporarily? Do you feel emptiness or emancipation? Do you feel conflict or comfort? Breathe into your family identity and notice what thoughts and feelings comes to mind. Be kind, honest and loving with yourself.

All these multifaceted identities, through unconscious bias and judgement can enhance, hold us back, disconnect or connect us from ourselves or others. Sometimes we are equally trying to protect our own identities furiously, hide behind them or try to justify them to others by seeking approval or acceptance. Whilst our multi-faceted identities are essential for personal growth and understanding of the world, for some of us, we can get wrapped up in our own identities and adopt or hold on to particular aspects that no longer serve us. Our identities are there to evolve and to emancipate and to enjoy and learn from, but paradoxically it can also imprison us and separate us from ourselves and our fellow human beings.

Identity

Our identities are just a set of beliefs, which are patterns of thoughts that we keep thinking about and hold on to again and again about ourselves and others. Therefore, our identity is based on beliefs. We become who we think we are, and so identities are personalities are formed. For example, I am a vegetarian as I was born into a family whose religious beliefs influenced the practice of vegetarianism. As I got older I had a choice to continue to be a vegetarian or not. Through life experiences and other influences, I have recently begun a journey with veganism. Our identities can be flexible, fluid and changeable and are forever evolving through our life experiences. The question is, are we allowing or resisting this expansion of our identities?

At our core essence, there are two key levels of identity: the 'outer me', and the 'inner me'. Whilst the 'outer me' identity is a complex gathering of our external conditioning, beliefs we hold and influences of our past and present experiences and memories. The 'inner me' is our true innate nature of infinite vibrational energy, that is unconditional love and limitless. Quantum physics would define our ultimate existence as a creative vibrational energy which is infinite and forever evolving in the physical world and onto the non-physical planes. We get a glimpse of this 'inner me' when we experience joy, love, satisfaction, compassion and appreciation and when we quieten the mind through mediation to suspend all thought. It is then that we are reminded that we are more than enough in the right now!

In essence, we are all beings of the universe and equal beyond our external identities. Each person brings their own unique diverse qualities and abilities that we choose to connect or disconnect with from time to time. We are one human race who continues to change and evolve in this lifetime. We have choices on the identities we like to hold onto, discard and create new ones. We are reminded that we are much more and beyond our external body, shape, gender, age, skin colour, name, and political, cultural or religious persuasions.

I am enough and more than who I think I am and forever evolving.

I AM EVOLUTION ME!

This chapter was inspired by the teachings of Abraham Hicks and Amanda Ellis podcast on: IDENTITY.

About Mina Kakaiya:

Mina is a social entrepreneur, mental health and wellbeing trainer, life coach and public speaker. She has a background in social work and over 20 years' experience in community development working in collaboration across health and social care NHS and not for profit sector and education in developing a diverse range of mental health and wellbeing projects and initiatives. She is involved in Influencing NHS service commissioning to improving health and social inequalities, for the wider population and those experiencing mental health problems and long term conditions. Mina is a mental health and MHFA (Mental Health First Aid), resilience in the workplace trainer and a mindfulness practioner. She has developed peer support training packages and services in Mental Health, HIV and Domestic Violence.

Mina holds a degree in Neuroscience and a Masters in CSR (Corporate Social Responsibility). She is passionate about promoting inner wellbeing towards personal transformation of individuals and communities.

Mina practices yoga and meditation and has a love for music and dance and interests in sustainable living and with a dream of building her own Eco home in the near future. She has her pink hard hat already!

For more information please connect with me on LinkedIn page.

CHAPTER EIGHT

You are a Beautiful Being, Capable of Creating Miracles In Your Life If You Just Believe In Yourself

By: Emma Di Gallo

Today we are being saturated by social media, exposed to how the most famous are living their dream lives. What we should look like or wear, what is the latest trend "everyone should follow", and who we should be in order to fit into today's society.

At home being the youngest of three, I always felt awkward due to being taller than my other siblings. I wasn't seeing and thinking like them. Instead I spent my time in my own imaginary world. I learned, at a young age, to take refuge in my own mind. Inventing a life that was abundant, exciting, full of adventure, but foremost love was everywhere. I always felt appreciated; it was basically a fairy tale life. The more the outer conditions become bleak the more I pushed myself to dream big, to dream bold. I saw myself in the future as a successful and happy young woman, smiling at the world while traveling.

I had an after-school tutor who was an old retired school teacher. I believed she was in her mid-60's... One day she looked at me with a solemn look on her face and told me "I can't help you anymore; there is nothing I can do for you!" My mother was so upset about it. I was a lost cause; someone whom at a very young age refused to read and writes. What kind of future could I have?

In high school our fate was already sealed, because my parents were blue collar the chance to attend higher education was nearly impossible. We, at the end of high school, had to pass some test that would reveled what we should be doing with our lives or at least what our aptitudes were. I do not recall the result of the test, but I do know leaving high school no paperwork was given to us to apply to University. Instead we were left to figure out what to do next.

When everyone thought I was a lost cause, I couldn't learn anything; I wasn't good enough, whatever the teachers were thinking I still knew that was not true. I always believe in myself no matter what the outer conditions were. I never took for granted what people where telling me. My warrior spirit never gave up instead I used the most powerful tool I had. It was my imagination pushing me to dream bolder.

My instinct was to continue to dream big, seeing myself living in a different country, traveling and enjoying who I was. I knew my life wasn't meant to be in Europe, but I had to have faith in the Universe to guide me and let perfect synchronicity work its magic.

It happened when an ad was placed by the Club Med in a newspaper. I responded to it and was selected for an interview. I went to Paris and with five other candidates in the same room we attended the interview. It was a little strange the way it happened but at the end of the interview I left to catch my train. I felt I failed the interview. I left Paris disappointed thinking I was not selected, I did not say a word to anyone about it. Couple of months later I received a call from them letting me know that they needed me in one of their villages. At first, I thought it was a joke and hung up but to my surprise they called me back. This was my opening, my ticket to leave that life that wasn't mine. I took the first step in the unknown and accepted the position.

It was the first step that guided me where I am today. I knew the Club Med was the incubator, the place where I needed to learn to be less shy and let my spirit be. Leaving my early, unhappy life behind me and be who I was meant to be. The fourth village I went to was in Italy. There I meet someone who was reading Dr Joseph Murphy's book, and she gave me one of his books. When I started to read it, I was stunned to realize that I was already using my mind to co-create with the Universe. I felt I was more connected than before; everything I was doing naturally came from a great place of wisdom. It was an "ah ha" moment that helped me along the way. I was still thinking about leaving Europe the opportunity finally came after my accident at the Club Med. I returned to stay with my sister while I was recovering I felt it was time for me to finally open my wings and fly away. It was the right time for me to leave Europe, synchronicity worked its magic I was finally on my way to the life I was meant to be living.

I kept dreaming but also opened my mind to learn, I started to work in corporate as a consultant. I learned most of my skills on the job; I let my curiosity wander around. It helped me to understand what others were doing. One thing I have taught myself to do is to learn from others, being opened to being taught other skill sets. Never stay in my line but instead empowering myself by understanding how corporations were operating. Expanding my wings opened the doors for me to a new level. I decided to unleash the full potential of my mind. For someone who has not had a formal education in computer science or business management I learned all of that by partnering with individuals that were more than happy to share their knowledge. I was able to become who I truly am, regardless of what the outer condition has been. My thirst for knowledge and understanding created unique opportunities. Everything I have done in my life has brought me where I am today. I created a new life, and I transformed myself like a butterfly. By shedding my old life for a new one, I reinvented who I am.

One gift I have had since I was born is that I am psychic. Through the years my gifts as a psychic strengthened, I was not only developing one skill but opening myself to the complexity of my soul, like a diamond letting each facet shine. I started to push the boundaries of my life to become limitless. By following the beat of my own drum, I pushed myself beyond what everyone thought I could do. Instead the fire in me pushed me beyond my wildest dreams. Learning at a young age to not let my outer condition influence me but instead giving me the spark, I needed to move mountains. Starting in the place where nothing was ever given to me on a "silver platter" but instead with my tenacity and strengths listening to the sound of my own drum, my beautiful spirit showed me everything was possible if you believe.

It may sound harsh and difficult for some of you to understand but it was a gift for me. I never saw myself as being beautiful or smarter than others, but instead it taught me to be honest and authentic. I never felt the need to seek out anyone's approval or being rescued. We learned through the hardship of our lives, but my spirit was relentless.

When everyone thought I was a lost cause, I couldn't learn anything, I wasn't good enough, whatever the teachers were thinking - I still knew that was not true.

I never listened to them; instead I continued to see myself as successful. Learning different languages, living an abundant life full of adventure, always on the go, I never had a moment of quietness. Instead I was on top of the world.

I kept that attitude after we had to move out of our house. I had no idea where I was going but I always had faith that I was on the right track and opportunity will come and knock at my door.

I never let the outer condition derail my imagination; I was always embodying those energies. As much as our situation was becoming bleak, I kept going, always dreaming, and projecting myself in a life of happiness and joy.

Living in a beautiful home, far away from where I was. By keeping that attitude, the Universe knew I wasn't going to give up, even at my worst. I refused to give up in what I believed in. I knew I did not belong where I was, but I needed to find that door.

We had to learn to relay on ourselves, always find ways to find solutions. This is what brought me here today. I was determined not to give up on myself and on my dreams. All these were achieved by learning new skills along my journey.

We are unique individuals; we are all living a different journey. I always walk to the beat of my own drum. I never liked conformity, I never fit in anyone's boxes but instead I use my uniqueness as a weapon for the greater good. I always saw myself as different from others because of my spirit. The way I think, I talk and walk makes me unique. We are all unique. We should not try to conform to society just because it may be safe for others.

Living my life through my spirit not my ego has opened the bounty from the universe. I have named and claimed everything I have done. The Universe in its perfect synchronicity has brought me everything I needed. I have never listened to social media, neither have I been letting anyone influence me on how I should live my life. Instead I have learned to ground myself and listen to my spirit.

My spirit has been my ally, my compass in good times and bad times. It taught me to navigate in the raging river that is my life. Learning to count my blessings, teaching me life lessons I needed to learn for me to move on in my journey. During trivial times, I have learned to lean on it, having faith that everything will be all right.

Through the heartache, I have learned that I was whole, I was enough. I did not feel the need to seek someone's approval instead I learned to stay authentic. The Universe in its infinite wisdom brought me during my life, the right people. Emulating someone else never came to mind. Instead I let my spirit be free, becoming who I am.

I had to face individual's that live their life through their ego. They never felt comfortable around me because I would not oblige nor conform to their expectations. As much as they tried to mold me in the shape they felt would be best. My warrior spirit never let it happen, from my personal to professional life. Instead I walked away from them freeing myself of the chains they tried to bind me with.

I have learned to live my life from my spirit, it is the purest form of experience you will ever have. Connecting with the universe, you are learning to realized we are all here to experience life, but also to connect with each other. Living a life of illusion through social media, and trying to conform to a society that doesn't allow us to live our lives through our spirits is the worst reality of the human race. Instead we must learn to accept and love who we are.

Each one of us is unique, we need to accept we are beautiful, magical and have love. The unconditional love you are feeling and experiencing when you are living your life through your spirit is the purest gold bond you will ever have. The energy you are emanating will bring you the right people and opportunities in your life. You cannot find this energy elsewhere.

If you are feeling insecure it is because you are letting your ego lead your life. If you let your ego lead your life you are feeling not worthy, beautiful, or whole. Instead you are seeking reassurance through others. Giving your power away to always try to please others will not do anything for your self-esteem. Feeling rejected, awkward, envious and jealous will poison your life. You are emanating negativity; the right people and situations will not come to you. Instead you need to tell your ego it is OK, you are safe and let your spirit lead your life.

If I had to believe everyone along my path that told me I wasn't good enough, not worthy or anything else along those lines, I would not have accomplished anything in my life, but instead I would have become "a victim" or a "martyr". I would be looking at my life passing by me, waiting for my time to die full of anger and resentment towards the world.

Instead, I decided to do whatever my instinct was inspiring me to become. Pushing my own limits, going beyond what I thought for me was impossible. Dreaming big, making things unfold for me. I believed in myself regardless of what people ever thought about me. I never looked at people for validation or approval. I never depended on anyone to give me their "two cents worth", especially when it was unwanted.

Words are powerful, if you are consciously or unconsciously telling a child or anyone as a matter of fact they are not worthy, you are robbing them of their true potential. Not everyone can learn at the same speed, some people are more inclined to learn faster than others. Some are more artistic than others. Whatever people can do, no one should set a limitation on them.

If I had listened to that teacher and my mother, I would not have traveled and lived in different countries. Neither would I have started to write a blog, a podcast show or created four websites on my own. I let my imagination inspire me. I have done everything I set my mind to do. I would like to emphasize, that I have listened to my instincts, that little voice inside of me who has been guiding me my entire life. I have always depended my personal compass (my Soul and light) to guide me on my journey.

Along my life I surrounded myself with a few people that I could trust, that would give me honest feedback. There is an old saying, if you have at least 3 people you can count on in your life, you are the luckiest person on Earth. You do not need to be surrounded by a court of people that do not have your best interests at heart.

If you listen closely when people speak you can figure out quickly if this comes from a place of good intentions or not. Also, it is not the words it is the intent. But when your soul is speaking to you, you know deep inside if this is right for you or not.

If someone is telling you 'You are not worthy' smile and let them be. Because everyone is worthy, we are all worthy no matter what. Don't let anyone rob you of who you are and what you are capable of doing. You do not need to be a genius or have a PHD to be worthy. Your uniqueness is what makes you precious.

I am living and breathing proof of that. There are millions of people around the world who are living their life to the fullest because they listened to their spirit. They believed in themselves because they are worthy. What's stopping you from doing the same? Is it because someone told you, you were not worthy or good enough? What could possibly validate that?

In todays' standards it feels like we should be turned into robots. But we are not, we are living spirits, we have our own free will. We should not let anyone dictate our lives. Instead we should be listening to our spirit. We are the essence of life, the pioneers, and the trailblazers. We are the creativity, the embodiment of life and unconditional love.

We are the inspiration for the next generation; we are the sparks that trigger positive changes into this world. Why should we be trading those beautiful energies for a life of misery?

We can have humble beginnings, but it doesn't mean we are not worthy! We do not need to be famous and posting our lives on social medias twenty-four by seven to feel worthy.

Instead we need to acknowledge our spirits wherever we are, from deep in the bush of Africa, the outback in Australia or in the middle of the concrete cities. We are the shining lights, the channel of love and positivity. We are the legacy that keeps the world changing and moving in the right direction. We are teaching each other it is never too late to change. We are not too old or too young to start to live our lives through our spirit.

One of the biggest lessons in life I have learned and applied is that no matter where you are born, what education you have you can co-create your life with the Universe. You can change the outer conditions and make what seems impossible, possible. Your imagination is the most powerful tool you have. Use it today to create the happy ending you want.

Listening to the beat of my own drum has brought me back home where I belong. I have learned so much along the way but foremost it inspired me today to share my story. As someone who has lived many lives using all the facets my spirit has, I have never given up on my dreams as a young child. I believed in me when no one else did. I knew deep in my core I had a long journey ahead to go home, to the life I was meant to live. I listened to the sound of my drum in the darkest times seeing myself protected and safe.

As we are all walking on our journey we should all take the time to listen to the sound of our own drum. It is our guide, our compass that guides us along the way. Even if for some of us the outer conditions are not ideal our imagination can help us change the course of our life for the best. It is never too late to start.

As you are reading my story start to listen to the beat of your own drum, it will guide you to uncharted territory living the life you are meant to live. Becoming limitless is not for the few chosen ones but everyone. Hold fast to your dreams and be bold. When you start to let your imagination run free this is where magic happens. You can change the course of your life to finally reach the bounty that is meant to be for you.

Tips:

Never give your power to someone else. Instead keep your head high, keep listening to your spirit.

Dream bold, let your imagination lead your life.

Stay authentic and grounded; create your own circle of light with people who are living their lives through their spirits.

Be grateful for what you have and continue to be the trailblazer.

Inspire others to live their life to the fullest.

Partner with the Universe to co-create the life you always wanted.

But foremost believe in yourself, never let anyone rain on your parade!

You are a beautiful being, capable of creating miracles in your life if you just believe in yourself.

About the author:

Emmanuelle Di Gallo is an international six sensory, psychic and a visionary guide. A wondrous raconteur, Emmanuelle is known for her enlightening humor; her laugh is contagious and will put you at ease. She is skilled in quickly shifting people from a state of worry to a clear positive energy. Because of her unique gifts Emmanuelle has helped countless individuals and companies over the years.

She is very well known to be the bridge that closes the gaps; she is a "fixer", a problem solver. Emmanuelle is sharing the Universe wisdom through her blog and has her own podcast show.

She is the founder of EDG & Associates, LLC; Emmanuelle describes her company as "East meets West".

It is multidimensional like her, it is not your "typical" consulting company also we are also focused on the utility world and regulatory, we have great speakers, writers, program managers and life coaches that provide unparalleled services.

www.edg-associates.com – www.edgintuitive.com

CHAPTER NINE

Loving Yourself Enough

Make it your passion

By Sarah Keen Post

"When your heart and mind align, you will be free to follow your passion and you will know your true purpose."

- Sarah Keen Post

12 years to a brand new you! Who wants to hear that? But such is the time frame of my story, my transformation. I began my journey not knowing where it would lead or how much it would literally change my life. Wanting to be healthy and active not only for myself but for my family, I made fitness, mental health and nutrition my top priority. I made MYSELF my top priority. By paying myself first every single day, I am a better person to and for the people I love, the people I spend my days with, for anyone I interact with. I can say that with confidence today, but only after overcoming severe anxiety that I internalized for years, made worse by insecurities about my weight and outer appearance. Knowing that I am not alone in these struggles has only made me more determined to use the experiences and knowledge I have gained to help and inspire others who are struggling as well.

My transformation has led to opportunities that I never imagined possible. In May of 2018, I had the honor of being a guest on a

Podcast. That Podcast is called *The Roots of Leadership* with Anthony Gruppo. Anthony is the CEO of the Northeast Region for Marsh & McLennan Agency. A true visionary leader, amazing author, incomparable motivator and passionate speaker, he not only sees strengths and skills in others that they haven't tapped into yet, but he sees an inner light that may have been dimmed, or maybe it's never been lit. He brings out the very best in the people he mentors, in anyone he meets. It was truly an amazing experience. It provided a platform for me to share my story, to reach out and let others know that I could relate to what they were going through. I've been there. Through this invaluable experience I came to realize that leadership has played a large part in my success.

As a result of that opportunity, I received many messages. Personal, all heartfelt, some of them heart wrenching, from people who related to my journey. I would like to share one of them with you now.

"I am reaching out to you because your Podcast moved me to tears. I thought it was amazing and very empowering. I am starting my journey tomorrow and I am telling you because I need to say it out loud to someone, so I do not have an excuse. I am tired. Tired of being invisible, I don't look in the mirror because I hate the person I've become. I want to be capable again, instead of self-doubting and in constant fear of what others think. I just needed to say my shit out loud, because I am carrying a lot of it. Thank you, friend."

That could have been written by me 12 years ago after the birth of my fifth child. Weighing 200 pounds, I looked in the mirror and said out loud "This is not acceptable." For me, my physical appearance wasn't acceptable, but also my mental mind-set wasn't acceptable. I was not being the Mom I wanted to be, and my quality of life was definitely not what I wanted it to be.

Along with the daily self-demeaning thoughts, I suffered from crippling anxiety. I had it, I have it. It robbed me of so many events, moments, travel, etc. It controlled me, I did not control it. I would go to the grocery store; a panic attack would ensue. I would leave an entire cart full in the aisle and walk out. I would not get my haircut for fear of getting half way through and what if I wanted to flee. The countless excuses that I made in order not to attend my kid's programs and event… When I did go somewhere, looking for exits, needing to know exactly where the bathrooms were, always planning my escape if needed. Also, the stories that I fabricated in order to avoid people and public places, and always praying that I would see no one I knew. Get in. Get out. Get home. That was my way of living. Wearing the same exact outfit day after day. Nothing mattered. I was merely existing. I was certainly not living. Even breathing was difficult at times.

All of those moments and events I mentioned, I fought through. I had to prove to myself that I could do it. Was it hard? Yes! My not going, not doing and not living my day to day life were affecting everything and everyone else in my life. Yes! But I realized I was responsible for more than just myself. With five busy children, there were sporting events, school programs and conferences to attend, just to name a few. Those events forced me to put myself out there, to appear in public where my feelings of anxiety and insecurity would only intensify. Even though my inner struggles were so intense, I appeared on the outside to have it all together. To anyone with anxiety, I feel you, I understand you. And I am here for you.

"Turn any negative thoughts into a positive, confident voice that speaks straight to your own heart."

- Sarah Keen Post

This leads me to where my transformation began. What motivated me? Honestly, I got mad, fed up, done. I was done taking the easy way out. I was done being a quitter. I was not going to let anxiety steal one more second of my life. My "This is not acceptable" attitude is what drove me. What else drove me? My children! They were, and still are my biggest motivation. It is so important to me to set a good example for them. I stayed at home with all five children. Lost in a routine of bottles, diapers, children's television programs, meal to meal, bedtime to bedtime, I lost myself to some extent. When did I shower last? Did I even sleep? Finding time for me was difficult to say the least, if not nearly impossible. What worked for me was to fly by the seat of my pants, moment to moment. I wasn't a planner mom, or a scheduled play date mom or a calendar mom. I guess the less strict of a schedule I kept, the lesser the stress. It was during those hectic years that I learned I am capable of far more than I thought I was. And after years of taking care of my kids, I know it is perfectly ok that now is *my time*. Time to show them that in my case, I can be a stay at home mom, then when they are all in school I can set goals for myself, achieve those goals and chase and live out my dreams.

"Focus and remember why you are doing what you are doing and who you are doing it for."

- Sarah Keen Post

Now that my kids are older, my lifestyle shows them that I value myself, my health and my mind. I want to be there for them and I want to be there for them for a long time. They have seen all the different stages of me. At a time when I didn't love myself, from them I learned unconditional love. Had I been able to see myself through their eyes, especially in the most difficult stages of my transformation, would I have been kinder to myself, more patient, knowing that it wasn't going to happen overnight? Would I have taken more cues from their hugs, I love yous and endless affection? Children are honest, there are no filters. They don't judge. They loved me always, loved me through it all, and are so proud of me now. It warms my heart and I am so incredibly proud of the caring, young woman and young men they are becoming.

"When you speak from your heart, you produce an authentic light,

a glow that can never be dimmed or put out by anyone. You are so very beautiful, keep shining."

- Sarah Keen Post

Family health history has also been a major motivator in my journey to become healthier in the long term. Wanting to do whatever I can to avoid serious health issues and multiple medications for various ailments in the future. Being consciously aware of my aging parents, observing their daily struggles, pain and frustration with the physical limitations they experience, has had a significant impact on me. I came to realize that making even small changes to my nutrition and activity level were gradually bringing me closer to that active life I was craving so badly. My previous sedentary, anxious lifestyle was slowly becoming a thing of the past, a closed chapter I never want to open again. While achieving my goals has not come without ups and downs, hills and valleys, wins and losses, and falling off the wagon more than once, the desire to change was stronger than remaining status quo. I wouldn't go to a gym until I thought I was presentable or respectable enough to show my face there. I worked out at home in my basement where no one could see me. Eventually, I ventured outside. I would walk around the block; I added to that each day-one step at a time.

"There is power in planning. There is wisdom in willpower. There is truth in tenacity. There is bravery in being bold. There is satisfaction in seeing it through."

- Sarah Keen Post

Did I have a vision for what I wanted to be, see, become? To some extent, yes! One thing I have always done is to set my sights and expectations high. This is what challenges me. My goals or vision may seem unattainable, ridiculous to some, but that pushes me to be my absolute best. I have never been more focused in my life than I am right now. Locked and loaded on my goals for the first time in forever. This equals results which produces determination. There is no stopping me. I lead myself to this place. I didn't know it at the time, but I had leadership skills and I discovered them in some of my weakest moments. How amazing is that?

"Stop for a moment. Focus. Breathe. Reset. Then carry on with a definite purpose and a clear vision."

- Sarah Keen Post

I say that I lead myself to this place, let me clarify. Did I have the inner strength, the determination, the willpower to get me here? Yes. Did I do the physical work? Yes. But did I surround myself with a team; did I find people that would support me, that wanted the very best for me, that would push me far beyond what I ever thought possible? Yes. These people gave me their time, their talents, their knowledge, their amazing skills, and asked for nothing in return. I am forever grateful to and for them. Your circle is crucial to your success. Choose wisely.

"Your dreams are only too big for those that are afraid you will make them come true."

- Sarah Keen Post

The people I just mentioned were, and remain, priceless resources for me. They are to this day there for me whenever I need them. I think back to my first trainer. He taught me the basics; he gave me a great foundation to build on. He instilled an amazing work ethic in me, and for that I am truly thankful. He also taught me to view food in a different way, as fuel for my body and not as an emotional indulgence or as a comfort. The food I fuel my body with makes it possible for it to perform the way that I want it to. Having my nutrition in check, along with my workouts, equalled results. Those results equalled motivation. This was a key component in my transformation. Be extremely grateful for the people that help you along the way. I have been so fortunate. They made a significant and lasting impact on me. I strive to be this same type of person to others. It was time to pay that forward.

"They don't know it yet, you don't know it yet. But someone out there needs what you have to give. Today may be the day you change a life."
- Sarah Keen Post

At a certain point, this stay at home mom of five could no longer afford a personal trainer. But I stayed committed, knowing that the knowledge I gained would never leave me. I will carry it with me always. No one can take that away. I am fairly confident that there isn't one thing that anyone going through a transformation has said to themselves that I haven't said to myself. I have beaten myself up. I have hated on myself. I have looked away from my reflection. I have wanted to give up, to quit. I have said, "What's the point?" But I didn't quit, which leads me to talk about passion. The definition of passion is *a strong and barely controllable emotion*. It becomes a part of you. Was it obsession? Yes! I can describe it as "Tunnel vision" - to some extent. Loving myself enough to take care of me became my passion.

Fitness and nutrition have become a passion for me, a way of life, a way to love life and live life to the fullest. The gym is my outlet, my therapy, my sanity. It is always there for me, it never lets me down. It gives me strength in so many ways, not just physical strength. You can see my physical transformation. You cannot see the mental transformation that has taken place. Whenever we discuss transformation, we cannot forget to reflect on the changes that happen within. The mental metamorphosis that one goes through is so incredibly important. The body and mind work together to get you where you ultimately want to go. Mind-set and Physical Strength must be in sync to produce results. It is an unbeatable combination. Staying focused, fiercely committed to my goals, never letting anyone discourage my vision, dreams or my fighting spirit, and keeps me strong. No one has the power to tell me that something can't be done.

"Tonight, I dream, tomorrow I do."
- Sarah Keen Post

Mind-set must transform with you. Your mind-set is also on a journey, sometimes a very bumpy one. It matters on the good days just as much as it matters, if not more on the bad days. Having the ability to bring yourself back from negative talk, thoughts and actions is crucial. I believe mental commitment precedes physical commitment. Mind-set is everything. Every single day, I am mentally at the gym before I physically walk through the doors. I mentally go through my workouts before I physically do them. I realize now that I had committed to a transformation in my mind, without even knowing what that meant at the time, and having no idea where my journey was headed. You have got to believe that you have it in you- because you do, and you are worth it.

"I want to see what is on the other side of discipline."
- Sarah Keen Post

My journey has taught me to judge no one. You do not know what they are going through, what they are suffering from or what thoughts are racing through their mind. You do not know why they do what they do; you have no clue as to why they are at the gym every day. Maybe they are running from something, maybe they are running to something or maybe they are just running. Don't question their methods or reasons. Whatever they need to do to come out on the other side, stronger, healthier, transformed, is their business. Encourage, support, and do not judge.

"Courageous can be doing something big. Courageous can be doing

something small. And all that matters is that you know whatever you did today, big or small, you ARE moving forward."

- Sarah Keen Post

Haven't we all asked ourselves, when will I be good enough? We must realize that the only person we have to be good enough for is ourselves. The only one we need to be better than is the person we were the day before. This is crucial to transformation. Strive to make yourself proud. Keep the promises that you make to yourself. You are the only one who knows why you do what you do. Remind yourself why you show up, why you put in the effort and why you are working so very hard. Stay inspired and use your motivation to inspire others. Any effort, any positive changes you make are valid and they matter. Look at your struggles as growth, as progress, a necessary component to your own transformation. Your struggles will shape you, they will strengthen you. Negative thoughts are not productive to your growth. Your mind, heart, body and soul are listening. Be caring, be kind and be confident. It all starts with you.

Accountability and consistency are keys to transformation. Never give up. Rest is ok, necessary and good for you. Rest, but do not ever quit. No matter where you are in your own personal journey, you are always so close to your next breakthrough. If you are feeling defeated, it means the struggle is bringing something big. Keep pushing. You are leveling up; it is not supposed to be easy. Forward you go; you are capable of far more than you know. Explore your potential. I dare you.

"New levels are empowering and exciting. When it is time to level up, you can feel it. It is a fire in you. Levels have no limits. Rise up."

- Sarah Keen Post

Here are some practical tips and techniques that I put together. I use them to regularly check myself throughout my day. How am

I REALLY doing, how am I feeling, what am I thinking, how am I talking to myself? Each day may be different, but you still own each day. Try your very best to keep your thoughts positive, productive and powerful.

Reminders:

- Pay yourself first.
- Move your body in some way every day.
- Plan ahead.
- Meal Prep.
- Drink your water.
- Get your rest.
- This is a lifestyle.
- Trust the process.
- Listen to your body.
- Don't let the scale make or break your day.
- You are worth it.
- You've got this.

Check yourself throughout the day:
Morning:

- Envision your day.
- Think about and plan your meals.
- Food is fuel.
- Drink your water.
- Plan a time to workout/move your body.

Noon:

- Are you drinking your water?
- Check your thoughts, attitude and mindset.
- Don't skip lunch.

- Take a few minutes to de-stress if you need it.
- Move your body for a few minutes too.

Night:

- You are committed to a workout today, don't cancel. You owe it to yourself.
- Something is better than nothing.
- Reflect on your day – Where did you excel? If you fall short on your journey, take note and do better tomorrow.
- Be gentle with yourself on your journey.
- Practice patience.
- Calm your thoughts at the end of the day.
- Meditate (if that works for you)

End of the week:

- How do you feel?
- How is your mindset?
- What areas do you need motivation?
- Take note of the small and the big victories, they all count.
- Congratulate yourself on your accomplishments.

I also encourage journaling; it doesn't have to be time consuming. Seeing your goals and vision in your own handwriting can make a big difference. Don't make this a stressful chore. Make it a time for you to reflect, reset and be ready for the next day. Keep it simple.

Know that you have a purpose. Be mindful that each phase, each stage, each level, teaches you something new. Embrace it and know that the best is yet to come. You are the one that will make it happen. You do not need validation from anyone to achieve greatness in your life. Loving yourself enough allows you to be your best self, benefitting both you and anyone around you. When you take the time to invest in your own personal health and well-being, the better equipped you are, physically and mentally, to handle the daily responsibilities and challenges that we all face. Never feel guilty for taking time for yourself, for caring for yourself, for being your own best friend and cheerleader at times. You are depending on you.

"Let your self-confidence shine. There is not one thing wrong with trusting in your own abilities. You have worked hard; use your experiences and knowledge to light the way for others."

- Sarah Keen Post

I am gradually coming to grips with how I've changed mentally and physically, trying not to think of it as the old me and the new me. I think about the people that only know me the way I am now, as well as the people who have seen all the stages of my transformation. I am a different person, I believe this. My mind-set, my confidence and my physical appearance have all been transformed. I carry myself differently. My posture is better. I am more self-assured, prouder, and more confident. Passing by a mirror now, I literally stop and think, "Is that really me?" I still struggle with self-confidence and body image issues. Losing a significant amount of weight can leave behind a significant amount of skin. But I consider that to be a part of my story, something that represents the struggle, the time, the effort, all the hard work, sweat and tears. I must admit, my body has been kind to me in my transformation, rebounding nicely, all things considered. Thank your body, you are amazing. Your body is made to move, it is meant for motion, and it is craving a change of pace. Show it some love, take that first step, and take that leap of faith.

"That leap of faith will lead you to what you are looking for, trust it. Take it. Tie your story together with your true purpose."

- Sarah Keen Post

If I were to have a conversation with Sarah from 12 years ago, what would I tell that woman now? I would sit across from her, no; I would sit right beside her, and tell her how proud I am of her. I would say there were times you never thought you could do it, but you did. I would tell her thank you. Without her strength, determination, and hard work, I wouldn't be where I am today. She fought through anxiety and made it out. She had faith in herself. She believed, and for that I am forever grateful. I would tell her that I love her.

"You will bloom in your own time, in your right moment. You will burst open and you will know that it was all worth the wait."

- Sarah Keen Post

12 years to a brand new you - Who wants to hear about it? I know not everyone would be interested. I have been asked what are you drinking, what are you eating, what are you doing? What is your secret? Besides a hell of a lot of hard work physically and mentally, I guess my secret all along was leadership. I AM a leader.

I have five children. I have a legacy to leave. I have a purpose. I am proud to say that I am no longer a quitter. No more not trying because what if something bad happens? What if I fail? What if they don't like me? No more. I am 47 and it is my time. It is never too late to do what you were born so long ago to do.

About Sarah Post:

Born in Iowa and now living in Nebraska, Sarah Keen Post is a mother of five who, at 47 years of age, successfully overcame twelve years of emotional and physical roadblocks to become a certified personal trainer and motivational speaker. Her mission is to use her personal experience and the knowledge she has gained in the field of fitness and health to inspire others to reach their wellness goals.

Finding it unacceptable to weigh 200 pounds following the birth of her fifth child in 2006, Sarah began a regimen of physical work and mental commitment to lose 77 pounds, reduce her body fat percentage considerably, and overcome crippling anxiety. Wanting to be healthy and active not only for herself but for her children, Sarah has made fitness, mental health and nutrition her top priorities. Her commitment to sharing her knowledge with others, not just about weight loss, but about overall health and wellness, is her passion.

Sarah offers advice and encouragement through social media and is currently serving as a coach and trainer for her personal clientele.

By sharing her transformational story, Sarah is confident that she can help others achieve their health and wellness goals and fulfill their dreams.

Lightning Source UK Ltd.
Milton Keynes UK
UKHW012008260219
338061UK00001B/13/P

9 781546 276180